Table Of Conten

Part one:

Part two: Low-Cholesterol Recipes

BREAKFAST OR BRANCH RECIPES

Soups and Stews

Side Dish

Fish and Seafood

Meat and Poultry

Salads

Vegetarian and Vegan Dishes

Mocktails & Smoothies
Mocktails

Smoothies

Deserts and Treats

Part Three: 30-Day Meal Plan

Part Four: Additional information

Introduction:

Welcome to the «Low Cholesterol Cookbook for Beginners,» your essential guide to navigating through the complexities of cholesterol management with ease and confidence. In today's world, where the diagnosis of high cholesterol is increasingly common, understanding how to control your cholesterol levels through diet is more important than ever. This condition does not discriminate; it can affect anyone, regardless of age, lifestyle, or background, making awareness and proactive management key to maintaining good health.

This cookbook is crafted to help those who are just beginning their journey towards a heart-healthy lifestyle and those who wish to maintain their well-being by keeping cholesterol levels in check. It's not just about limiting certain foods; it's about embracing a diverse, nutritious, and delicious diet that can positively impact your health.

The prevalence of high cholesterol in our communities underscores the importance of accessible and practical dietary strategies. That's why, before we explore the myriad of tasty and healthful recipes this book offers, we'll start with a foundational understanding of cholesterol. The upcoming chapter, «What Is Cholesterol?» will provide you with essential insights into the nature of cholesterol, its effects on the body, and why a cholesterol-conscious diet is crucial for preventing and managing this widespread health concern.

With this knowledge, you'll see how each recipe in this cookbook is not just a meal but a step towards a healthier heart and a better quality of life.

What Is Cholesterol?

Welcome to the introductory chapter of our exploration into the intricate world of cholesterol. Beyond its surface, cholesterol reveals a nuanced story of essential functions, intricate pathways, and the delicate balance that shapes our cardiovascular health.

Cholesterol is a waxy, fat-like substance found in every body cell.
Cholesterol, often misunderstood as an adversary, is, in fact, a fundamental molecule. It serves as a structural component of cell membranes, aiding in their stability and fluidity, producing hormones, and aiding in the digestion of fat, which are crucial for the proper functioning of our bodies. Additionally, cholesterol is a precursor for synthesizing essential molecules such as vitamin D.
While cholesterol is necessary for various bodily functions, excess can pose significant health risks.

Cholesterol, its types

Types of Cholesterol: LDL and HDL
Two primary players emerge within the realm of cholesterol: Low–Density Lipoprotein (LDL) and High-Density Lipoprotein (HDL). These distinct types dictate the delicate equilibrium between cholesterol metabolism's constructive and potentially harmful aspects.

LDL - The Intricate Carrier:

Often dubbed the «bad» cholesterol, LDL transports cholesterol from the liver to cells throughout the body. However, an excess of LDL can accumulate cholesterol in the arterial walls, contributing to atherosclerosis and increasing the risk of cardiovascular diseases.

HDL - The Protective Escort:

On the contrary, HDL, or the «good» cholesterol, functions as a protective escort, carrying excess cholesterol away from the cells and back to the liver. This process prevents the buildup of cholesterol in arteries, reducing the risk of heart-related issues.

A Symphony of Balance

The dynamic interplay between LDL and HDL cholesterol forms a symphony within our bodies. Achieving and maintaining a delicate balance is essential for cardiovascular health.

Causes of high cholesterol

Understanding the causes of high cholesterol is crucial for managing and preventing associated health risks. A variety of factors can influence cholesterol levels in the body:

Nutrition:

The most influential factor is your diet. Eating foods high in saturated fats, trans fats, and cholesterol can raise blood cholesterol levels. These include fatty meats, full-fat dairy products, fried foods... On the other hand, foods rich in unsaturated fats, like avocados, nuts, and olive oil, can help manage cholesterol levels.

Physical Inactivity:

Lack of exercise or a sedentary lifestyle can lower HDL (good) cholesterol levels. Regular physical activity can help raise HDL cholesterol and remove LDL (bad) cholesterol from the bloodstream.

Obesity:

Carrying excess weight tends to raise LDL cholesterol and lower HDL cholesterol. Losing weight can help correct these imbalances.

Age and Gender:

As you age, your body's chemistry changes, often increasing cholesterol levels. Before menopause, women generally have lower total cholesterol levels than men of the same age, but after menopause, women's LDL levels often rise.

Genetics:

Your genetic makeup can affect how your body processes cholesterol and fats. Familial hypercholesterolemia is a condition that causes high LDL cholesterol levels and can lead to early heart disease.

Smoking:
Smoking damages blood vessels, making them more susceptible to the accumulation of fatty deposits. Additionally, smoking may lower HDL cholesterol.

Alcohol Consumption:
Excessive alcohol intake can lead to serious health problems, including higher levels of triglycerides and high blood pressure.

Health Conditions:
Certain medical conditions, such as diabetes, hypothyroidism, and liver or kidney disease, can affect cholesterol levels.
For example, diabetes often lowers HDL cholesterol and raises LDL cholesterol and triglycerides. Hypothyroidism can lead to elevated cholesterol levels, as can kidney and liver diseases.

The Role of Medications: Some medications, including certain types of birth control, steroids, and diuretics, can affect cholesterol levels. It's important to discuss these effects with your healthcare provider.

Symptoms of high cholesterol Understanding the Silent Risk

High cholesterol itself typically doesn't have any symptoms. In most cases, people don't realize their cholesterol level is too high until they undergo a blood test or develop complications, such as heart disease or a stroke. This is why high cholesterol is often referred to as a «silent» condition. However, understanding the potential indicators and related conditions can be crucial for early detection and management.

Indirect Symptoms and Related Conditions:

Heart Disease: The most common consequence of high cholesterol is heart disease. Symptoms of heart disease include chest pain (angina), headaches, shortness of breath, and fatigue, especially during physical activity.

Stroke: A stroke, which can occur when a blood clot blocks blood flow to a part of your brain, might be a sign of high cholesterol. Symptoms of a stroke include sudden numbness or weakness in the face, arm, or leg, especially on one side of the body, confusion, trouble speaking, difficulty seeing, dizziness, or loss of balance. Peripheral Arterial Disease (PAD): PAD, caused by narrowed arteries in your limbs due to cholesterol buildup, can lead to leg pain when walking, numbness, or coldness in your lower legs or feet.

Xanthomas: In some cases, high cholesterol leads to fatty skin deposits known as xanthomas. These can appear as yellowish patches around the eyelids or lumps in other body parts.

The Importance of Regular Screening:
Regular cholesterol screenings are vital since high cholesterol is often asymptomatic until serious complications arise. The American Heart Association recommends that adults age 20 and older have their cholesterol levels checked every four to six years. More frequent testing might be necessary if you have a family history of high cholesterol or heart disease or if you have other risk factors such as smoking, diabetes, or high blood pressure.

While high cholesterol may not show obvious symptoms, managing it is crucial for long-term health. A combination of a healthy diet, regular physical activity, maintaining a healthy weight, and possibly medication can effectively manage cholesterol levels. This cookbook provides recipes and tips to help you on this journey, focusing on heart-healthy ingredients and lifestyle choices.

CUTTING CHOLESTEROL
Simple and Effective Strategies

High cholesterol can be a significant risk factor for heart disease and stroke. The good news is that it's often possible to lower cholesterol levels and reduce these risks through diet, lifestyle changes, and, when necessary, medication. Here's a deeper look at effective strategies for cutting cholesterol:

Daily Dietary Recommendations for Managing High Cholesterol.

Nutrition:

Fruits and Vegetables:
Aim for 400-500 grams (14-18 ounces) of fruits and vegetables daily, divided into 4-5 servings. For example, one medium apple is approximately 150 grams (5.3 ounces).

Whole Grains:
Include around 90-120 grams (3-4 ounces) of whole grains daily, which equates to 2-3 servings. One serving might be a slice of whole-grain bread (30 grams or 1 ounce) or half a cup of cooked brown rice (100 grams or 3.5 ounces).

Lean Proteins:
Aim for 85-170 grams (3-6 ounces) daily for meat and poultry. For fish, target at least two servings per week, with one serving around 140 grams (5 ounces).
For plant-based proteins like beans and lentils, a serving is about 150 grams (5.3 ounces) cooked.

Low-Fat Dairy:

Opt for low-fat or non-fat dairy products. This includes milk, yogurt, and cheese that are low in fat. Consumption Amount: Having 1-2 servings of dairy products is recommended daily. One serving could be, for example, one glass of milk, a small yogurt, or 30 grams of cheese.

Healthy Fats:

Include healthy fats, but limit total fat intake to about 40-70 grams per day (1.4-2.5 ounces), focusing on monounsaturated and polyunsaturated fats.

Nuts and Seeds:

A serving of nuts is about 30 grams (1 ounce), roughly a small handful. Aim for 3-4 servings per week.

Hydration:

Drink at least 2 liters (about 68 ounces) of water daily.

Limiting Unhealthy Foods:

• Limit to 85 grams (3 ounces) per serving of red meat and no more than 1-2 servings per week.
• Minimize high-sugar foods, aiming for less than 25 grams (0.9 ounces) of added sugar daily.
• Minimize intake of processed and fried foods.
• Adults should limit their salt intake to less than 5 grams (around 0.18 ounces) daily.
• Eliminate fast food.
• Be mindful of portion sizes to manage calorie intake and maintain a healthy weight.
• Hydration: Drink plenty of water throughout the day. Aim for 8-10 glasses of water daily.

This guide provides a framework, but individual needs may vary. Consult with a healthcare provider or a dietitian for personalized advice.

Pear and Walnut Overnight Oats

Ingredients:

 4 servings |  10 minutes |  0 minutes

- 1 cup rolled oats
- 1 cup unsweetened almond milk
- 1 cup low-fat Greek yogurt
- 2 tablespoons honey
- 1 teaspoon vanilla extract
- 1/2 teaspoon ground cinnamon
- 2 medium pears, diced
- 1/4 cup chopped walnuts
- Additional honey or maple syrup for serving (optional)

Directions:

1. Mix the rolled oats, almond milk, Greek yogurt, honey, vanilla extract, and ground cinnamon in a large bowl.
2. Stir in the diced pears.
3. Divide the mixture into four serving jars or containers.
4. Cover and refrigerate overnight (or for at least 6 hours).
5. Before serving, stir the oats and top with chopped walnuts.
6. Drizzle with additional honey or maple syrup if desired.
7. erve chilled.

This recipe offers a balanced and nutritious start to the day, particularly for those managing cholesterol levels. Using low-fat Greek yogurt and unsweetened almond milk helps keep cholesterol levels low.

Nutritional Information: (per serving, approximate) Calories: 250, Protein: 9g, Carbohydrates: 44g, Fat: 6g, Fiber: 6g, Cholesterol: 5mg, Sodium: 55mg, Potassium: 270mg.

Mediterranean Veggie Breakfast Bowl

Ingredients:

 4 servings | 10 minutes | 20 minutes

- 2 cups fresh spinach
- 1 cup cherry tomatoes, halved
- 1 medium zucchini, diced
- 1 red bell pepper, diced
- 1/2 cup Kalamata olives, pitted and halved
- 1 cup cooked quinoa
- 1 tablespoon olive oil
- 1 teaspoon dried oregano
- Salt and pepper to taste
- 1 avocado, sliced
- 4 tablespoons hummus
- Optional: lemon wedges for serving

Directions:

1. Heat the olive oil in a large skillet over medium heat. Add the zucchini and bell pepper, sauteing until they soften, about 5-7 minutes.
2. Add the cherry tomatoes and Kalamata olives to the skillet. Continue to cook for 3-5 minutes until the tomatoes are soft.
3. Stir in the fresh spinach and cook until it wilts, about 2 minutes. Season the vegetable mixture with dried oregano, salt, and pepper.
4. Divide the cooked quinoa into four bowls. Top each bowl with an equal portion of the sautéed vegetable mixture.
5. Place a tablespoon of hummus on top of the veggies in each bowl and garnish with sliced avocado.
6. Serve each bowl with a lemon wedge on the side, if desired.

This Mediterranean Veggie Breakfast Bowl is a vibrant and nutritious start to the day, combining wholesome vegetables with quinoa for a filling, low-cholesterol meal. Topped with creamy hummus and fresh avocado, it's a perfect example of a heart-healthy breakfast that doesn't compromise on flavor or satisfaction.

Nutritional Information (per serving, approximate): Calories: 250, Protein: 8 g, Carbohydrates: 30 g, Fat: 12 g, Fiber: 7 g, Cholesterol: 0 mg, Sodium: 300 mg, Potassium: 600 mg

Whole-Grain Toast with Ricotta and Sliced Strawberries

 2 servings    5 minutes    2 minutes

Ingredients:

- 2 slices whole-grain bread
- 1/2 cup low-fat ricotta cheese
- 1 cup sliced fresh strawberries
- Honey or agave syrup (optional)

Directions:

1. Toast the whole-grain bread slices to your desired crispness.
2. Spread the ricotta cheese evenly over each slice of toast.
3. Top the ricotta with sliced strawberries.
4. Drizzle with honey or agave syrup, if desired.
5. Serve immediately.

This simple and nutritious recipe offers a delightful combination of flavors and textures, making it a perfect low-cholesterol breakfast or snack.

Nutritional Information: (per serving, approximate) Calories: 210, Protein: 11g, Carbohydrates: 27g, Fat: 7g, Fiber: 5g, Cholesterol: 20mg, Sodium: 200mg, Potassium: 300mg.

Baked Avocado Eggs with Bell Pepper

 2 servings   5 minutes   15 minutes

Ingredients:

- 1 ripe avocado
- 2 large eggs
- 1/2 red bell pepper, diced
- Salt and pepper to taste
- Fresh parsley or chives for garnish (optional)

Directions:

1. Preheat oven to 425°F (220°C).
2. Halve the avocado and remove the pit. Scoop out a little extra avocado to make room for the egg.
3. Place avocado halves in a baking dish to prevent them from tipping.
4. Crack an egg into each avocado half. Top with diced bell pepper.
5. Season with salt and pepper.
6. Bake for 14-16 minutes or until the eggs are cooked to your liking.
7. Garnish with fresh parsley or chives, if desired.

This recipe offers a heart-healthy and delicious breakfast option that combines the good fats of avocado with the protein of eggs, perfect for those managing cholesterol levels.

Nutritional Information: (per serving, approximate) Calories: 220, Protein: 8g, Carbohydrates: 9g, Fat: 18g, Fiber: 7g, Cholesterol: 185mg, Sodium: 70mg, Potassium: 540mg.

Pumpkin Spice Quinoa Porridge

 4 servings   5 minutes   20 minutes

Ingredients:

- 1 cup quinoa, rinsed
- 2 cups unsweetened almond milk
- 1 cup canned pumpkin puree
- 2 tablespoons maple syrup
- 1 teaspoon ground cinnamon
- 1/2 teaspoon ground ginger
- 1/4 teaspoon ground nutmeg
- 1/4 teaspoon ground cloves (optional)
- Pinch of salt
- Chopped nuts and additional almond milk for serving (optional)

Directions:

1. Combine quinoa and almond milk in a saucepan. Bring to a boil over medium heat.
2. Reduce heat to low, cover, and simmer for 15 minutes until most liquid is absorbed.
3. Stir in pumpkin puree, maple syrup, cinnamon, ginger, nutmeg, cloves, and a pinch of salt.
4. Cook for an additional 5 minutes, stirring occasionally.
5. Serve warm, topped with chopped nuts and a splash of almond milk if desired.

This warming and nutritious porridge is perfect for a low-cholesterol breakfast, offering a delicious way to start the day with the health benefits of quinoa and pumpkin.

Nutritional Information: (per serving, approximate) Calories: 210, Protein: 6g, Carbohydrates: 39g, Fat: 4g, Fiber: 5g, Cholesterol: 0mg, Sodium: 80mg, Potassium: 300mg.

Spinach and Feta Breakfast Burrito

 4 servings  10 minutes   10 minutes

Ingredients:

- 4 large eggs
- 1/4 cup low-fat milk
- 2 cups fresh spinach, chopped
- 1/2 cup crumbled feta cheese
- 4 whole-grain tortillas
- Salt and pepper to taste
- Cooking spray or olive oil

Directions:

1. In a bowl, whisk together eggs and milk. Season with salt and pepper.
2. Heat a non-stick skillet over medium heat. Lightly coat with cooking spray or olive oil.
3. Add the egg mixture to the skillet and scramble until set.
4. Stir in the chopped spinach, cooking until wilted.
5. Remove from heat and sprinkle feta cheese over the eggs.
6. Divide the egg mixture evenly among the tortillas.
7. Roll up the tortillas, folding the sides to enclose the filling.

This Spinach and Feta Breakfast Burrito offers a tasty and satisfying low-cholesterol meal, combining the protein of eggs with the goodness of spinach and whole grains.

Nutritional Information: (per serving, approximate) Calories: 280, Protein: 15g, Carbohydrates: 23g, Fat: 14g, Fiber: 3g, Cholesterol: 195mg, Sodium: 460mg, Potassium: 200mg.

Apple Cinnamon Baked Oatmeal

 6 servings  10 minutes 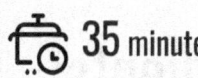 35 minutes

Ingredients:

- 2 cups rolled oats
- 1 1/2 teaspoons ground cinnamon
- 1 teaspoon baking powder
- 1/4 teaspoon salt
- 2 cups unsweetened almond milk
- 1/4 cup maple syrup
- 1 large apple, cored and diced
- 1/2 cup chopped walnuts
- 1 egg, beaten

Directions:

1. Preheat oven to 375°F (190°C). Grease a baking dish.
2. Mix oats, cinnamon, baking powder, and salt in a large bowl.
3. Add almond milk, maple syrup, diced apple, walnuts, and beaten egg. Stir until combined.
4. Pour the mixture into the prepared baking dish.
5. Bake for 35 minutes until the top is golden and the oats are set.
6. Let cool slightly before serving.

This wholesome Apple Cinnamon-Baked Oatmeal is a heart-healthy, perfect breakfast option for those managing cholesterol levels. It offers a delicious blend of flavors and nutrients.

Nutritional Information: (per serving, approximate) Calories: 220, Protein: 6g, Carbohydrates: 32g, Fat: 8g, Fiber: 5g, Cholesterol: 30mg, Sodium: 150mg, Potassium: 200mg.

Apple Barley and Berry Breakfast Salad

 4 servings  10 minutes 40 minutes

Ingredients:

- 1 cup barley
- 2 cups water
- 1 large apple, diced
- 1/2 cup fresh blueberries
- 1/2 cup fresh strawberries, sliced
- 1/4 cup chopped walnuts
- 2 tablespoons lemon juice
- 1 tablespoon honey
- 1/2 teaspoon cinnamon

Directions:

1. Rinse barley under cold water. In a pot, bring barley and water to a boil. Reduce heat, cover, and simmer for 40 minutes.
2. Once barley is cooked, let it cool to room temperature.
3. Combine cooked barley, diced apple, blueberries, strawberries, and chopped walnuts in a large bowl.
4. Whisk together lemon juice, honey, and cinnamon in a small bowl.
5. Pour the dressing over the salad and toss to combine.
6. Serve the salad chilled or at room temperature.

This recipe offers a nutritious and refreshing low-cholesterol breakfast option that combines the hearty texture of barley with the sweetness of fresh fruits and the crunch of walnuts.

Nutritional Information: (per serving, approximate) Calories: 220, Protein: 5g, Carbohydrates: 45g, Fat: 4g, Fiber: 8g, Cholesterol: 0mg, Sodium: 10mg, Potassium: 280mg.

Savory Mushroom and Zucchini Pancakes

 4 servings  15 minutes 10 minutes

Ingredients:

- 1 cup shredded zucchini
- 1 cup chopped mushrooms
- 2 green onions, finely chopped
- 2 large eggs
- 1/2 cup whole wheat flour
- 1/4 teaspoon garlic powder
- Salt and pepper to taste
- Olive oil for cooking

Directions:

1. Squeeze excess moisture from the shredded zucchini using a clean towel.
2. Combine zucchini, mushrooms, green onions, eggs, flour, garlic powder, salt, and pepper in a bowl. Mix well.
3. Heat a non-stick skillet over medium heat and lightly coat with olive oil.
4. Scoop 1/4 cup of batter for each pancake onto the skillet. Flatten slightly.
5. Cook for 3-4 minutes on each side until golden brown.
6. Serve warm.

These savory pancakes are a delightful low-cholesterol breakfast option, combining the flavors of mushrooms and zucchini with a hint of garlic, perfect for a nutritious start to the day.

Nutritional Information: (per serving, approximate) Calories: 140, Protein: 6g, Carbohydrates: 15g, Fat: 6g, Fiber: 3g, Cholesterol: 95mg, Sodium: 150mg, Potassium: 300mg.

Whole-Grain Waffles with Blueberry Compote

 4 servings  15 minutes  20 minutes

Ingredients:

- 1 cup whole wheat flour
- 1/2 cup rolled oats
- 2 teaspoons baking powder
- 1/4 teaspoon salt
- 1 egg
- 1 1/4 cups skim milk
- 2 tablespoons vegetable oil
- 1 teaspoon vanilla extract
- 2 cups fresh blueberries
- 2 tablespoons honey

Directions:

1. Mix flour, oats, baking powder, and salt in a bowl.
2. Whisk together egg, milk, oil, and vanilla in another bowl.
3. Combine wet and dry ingredients and mix until smooth.
4. Preheat a waffle iron and cook waffles according to the manufacturer's instructions.
5. Combine blueberries and honey in a saucepan over medium heat for the compote. Cook until berries burst and create a sauce, about 10 minutes.
6. Serve waffles topped with blueberry compote.

These whole-grain waffles with homemade blueberry compote provide a heart-healthy breakfast option. They are rich in fiber and antioxidants and perfect for those managing cholesterol levels.

Nutritional Information: (per serving, approximate) Calories: 300, Protein: 10g, Carbohydrates: 50g, Fat: 8g, Fiber: 6g, Cholesterol: 50mg, Sodium: 300mg, Potassium: 200mg.

Multigrain Porridge with Dried Fruits and Nuts

 4 servings  5 minutes  20 minutes

Ingredients:

- 1/2 cup rolled oats
- 1/2 cup quinoa
- 1/2 cup millet
- 4 cups water
- 1/4 cup chopped dried fruits (e.g., apricots, raisins)
- 1/4 cup chopped nuts (e.g., almonds, walnuts)
- Honey or maple syrup to taste (optional)

Directions:

1. Rinse quinoa and millet under cold water.
2. Combine oats, quinoa, millet, and water in a large saucepan. Bring to a boil.
3. Reduce heat to low and simmer for 20 minutes, stirring occasionally.
4. Once cooked, stir in dried fruits and nuts.
5. Sweeten with honey or maple syrup if desired.
6. Serve warm.

This hearty multigrain porridge is a nutritious, low-cholesterol breakfast option, enriched with the goodness of dried fruits and nuts, perfect for a wholesome start to the day.

Nutritional Information: (per serving, approximate) Calories: 300, Protein: 10g, Carbohydrates: 50g, Fat: 8g, Fiber: 6g, Cholesterol: 0mg, Sodium: 10mg, Potassium: 300mg.

Baked Sweet Potato and Kale Hash

 4 servings  15 minutes  25 minutes

Ingredients:

- 2 large sweet potatoes, diced
- 2 cups kale, chopped
- 1 red onion, diced
- 2 cloves garlic, minced
- 2 tablespoons olive oil
- Salt and pepper to taste
- 1/4 teaspoon paprika (optional)

Directions:

1. Preheat oven to 400°F (200°C).
2. In a large bowl, toss sweet potatoes, kale, onion, and garlic with olive oil, salt, pepper, and paprika.
3. Spread the mixture on a baking sheet.
4. Bake for 25 minutes, stirring halfway through, until sweet potatoes are tender.
5. Serve hot.

This delicious and nutritious hash is perfect for a low-cholesterol diet, combining the health benefits of sweet potatoes and kale with a savory blend of spices.

Nutritional Information: (per serving, approximate) Calories: 200, Protein: 3g, Carbohydrates: 35g, Fat: 7g, Fiber: 5g, Cholesterol: 0mg, Sodium: 70mg, Potassium: 600mg.

Smoked Salmon and Avocado on Whole-Grain Bagel

 2 servings   5 minutes  0 minutes

Ingredients:

- 2 whole-grain bagels, halved
- 4 ounces smoked salmon
- 1 ripe avocado, sliced
- 1 tablespoon capers (optional)
- Fresh dill for garnish (optional)
- Freshly ground black pepper

Directions:

1. Toast the bagel halves until golden and crispy.
2. Layer each bagel half with smoked salmon and avocado slices.
3. Sprinkle with capers and dill if using.
4. Season with freshly ground black pepper.
5. Serve immediately.

This nutritious and satisfying breakfast combines the rich flavors of smoked salmon and avocado on a hearty whole-grain bagel, perfect for a low-cholesterol diet.

Nutritional Information: (per serving, approximate) Calories: 400, Protein: 20g, Carbohydrates: 50g, Fat: 15g, Fiber: 7g, Cholesterol: 10mg, Sodium: 600mg, Potassium: 500mg.

Cranberry Orange Quinoa and Millet Granola

 6 servings  10 minutes   30 minutes

Ingredients:

- 2 cups rolled oats
- 1/2 cup quinoa, uncooked
- 1/2 cup millet, uncooked
- 1/2 cup dried cranberries
- Zest of 1 orange
- 1/4 cup honey or maple syrup
- 1/4 cup vegetable oil
- 1/2 teaspoon vanilla extract
- Pinch of salt

Directions:

1. Preheat oven to 300°F (150°C).
2. Combine oats, quinoa, millet, cranberries, and orange zest in a large bowl.
3. Mix honey, oil, vanilla extract, and salt in another bowl.
4. Pour the wet ingredients into the dry ingredients and mix well.
5. Spread the granola mixture evenly on a baking sheet.
6. Bake for 30 minutes, stirring halfway through, until golden and crisp.
7. Let cool before serving.

This Cranberry Orange Mixed Grain Granola is a delicious and nutritious low-cholesterol breakfast option, perfect for adding a crunch to your morning routine.

Nutritional Information: (per serving, approximate) Calories: 300, Protein: 7g, Carbohydrates: 45g, Fat: 10g, Fiber: 5g, Cholesterol: 0mg, Sodium: 50mg, Potassium: 250mg.

Banana and Walnut Whole-Grain Muffins

Ingredients:

- 1 1/2 cups whole wheat flour
- 1/2 cup rolled oats
- 1/3 cup honey or maple syrup
- 1/3 cup vegetable oil
- 2 ripe bananas, mashed
- 2 large eggs
- 1/4 cup milk
- 1 teaspoon baking powder
- 1/2 teaspoon baking soda
- 1/2 teaspoon vanilla extract
- 1/2 cup chopped walnuts
- Pinch of salt

 6 servings | 15 minutes | 20 minutes

Directions:

1. Preheat oven to 350°F (175°C). Line a muffin tin with paper liners.
2. Mix flour, oats, baking powder, baking soda, and salt in a large bowl.
3. Mix mashed bananas, eggs, oil, milk, honey, and vanilla extract in another bowl.
4. Combine wet and dry ingredients, stirring until just mixed.
5. Fold in chopped walnuts.
6. Divide batter into muffin cups.
7. Bake for 20 minutes or until a toothpick inserted into the center comes clean.

These wholesome muffins are an excellent low-cholesterol breakfast or snack option, combining the heart-healthy benefits of whole grains, bananas, and walnuts.

Nutritional Information: (per serving, approximate) Calories: 310, Protein: 7g, Carbohydrates: 45g, Fat: 14g, Fiber: 4g, Cholesterol: 60mg, Sodium: 200mg, Potassium: 250mg.

Veggie-Stuffed Breakfast Bell Peppers

Ingredients:

- 4 bell peppers, tops removed and seeded
- 4 large eggs
- 1 cup spinach, chopped
- 1/2 cup cherry tomatoes, halved
- 1/4 cup red onion, finely chopped
- Salt and pepper to taste
- 1/4 cup low-fat shredded cheese (optional)

 4 servings | 15 minutes | 25 minutes

Directions:

1. Preheat oven to 350°F (175°C). Place bell peppers upright in a baking dish.
2. Layer spinach, cherry tomatoes, and red onion in each pepper.
3. Crack an egg into each pepper.
4. Season with salt and pepper.
5. Sprinkle with shredded cheese if using.
6. Bake for 25 minutes or until eggs are set.
7. Serve hot.

These Veggie-Stuffed Breakfast Bell Peppers are a colorful and nutritious low-cholesterol breakfast option, perfect for a hearty and healthy start to the day.

Nutritional Information: (per serving, approximate) Calories: 150, Protein: 10g, Carbohydrates: 12g, Fat: 7g, Fiber: 3g, Cholesterol: 185mg, Sodium: 150mg, Potassium: 350mg.

Zucchini and Carrot Fritters with Yogurt Dip

 4 servings |  15 minutes | 10 minutes

Ingredients:

- 2 medium zucchinis, grated
- 2 medium carrots, grated
- 1/4 cup whole wheat flour
- 2 large eggs
- Salt and pepper to taste
- Olive oil for cooking
- 1 cup low-fat Greek yogurt
- 1 tablespoon fresh dill, chopped
- 1 clove garlic, minced

Directions:

1. Squeeze excess moisture from grated zucchini and carrots using a clean towel.
2. Combine zucchini, carrots, flour, eggs, salt, and pepper in a bowl.
3. Heat olive oil in a skillet over medium heat.
4. Scoop the mixture into the skillet, forming small fritters. Flatten slightly.
5. Cook each side for 3-4 minutes until golden brown.
6. Mix Greek yogurt with dill and minced garlic for the dip.
7. Serve fritters hot with yogurt dip on the side.

These Zucchini and Carrot Fritters are a delicious and nutritious low-cholesterol breakfast option, served with a healthy and flavorful yogurt dip.

Low Cholesterol Yogurt Dip

Ingredients:

- 1 cup low-fat Greek yogurt
- 1 tablespoon fresh dill, chopped
- 1 clove garlic, minced
- Salt and pepper to taste

Directions:

1. Combine the Greek yogurt, chopped dill, and minced garlic in a small bowl.
2. Season with salt and pepper to taste.
3. Mix well until all ingredients are thoroughly combined.
4. Refrigerate until ready to serve with the fritters.
5. This Yogurt Dip is perfect for a low-cholesterol diet, offering a creamy and flavorful complement to the Zucchini and Carrot Fritters or other dishes.

Nutritional Information: (per serving, approximate) Calories: 160, Protein: 10g, Carbohydrates: 18g, Fat: 6g, Fiber: 3g, Cholesterol: 95mg, Sodium: 120mg, Potassium: 400mg.

Sweet Potato and Black Bean Breakfast Burrito

Ingredients:

- 1 large sweet potato, peeled and diced
- 1 can black beans, drained and rinsed
- 4 whole-grain tortillas
- 1/2 cup low-fat shredded cheese
- 1 avocado, sliced
- 1/2 red onion, diced
- 1 teaspoon olive oil
- Salt and pepper to taste
- 1/2 teaspoon cumin
- Salsa for serving (optional)

 4 servings    15 minutes    20 minutes

Directions:

1. Heat olive oil in a skillet. Add sweet potatoes, cumin, salt, and pepper. Cook until tender, about 15 minutes.
2. Add black beans and red onion. Cook for another 5 minutes.
3. Warm tortillas in a separate skillet or microwave.
4. Assemble burritos: spoon sweet potato and bean mixture onto tortillas and top with cheese and avocado slices.
5. Roll up tortillas, folding in the sides.
6. Serve with salsa if desired.

This Sweet Potato and Black Bean Breakfast Burrito offers a hearty and nutritious start to the day, packed with fiber and protein, and perfect for a low-cholesterol diet.

Nutritional Information: (per serving, approximate) Calories: 350, Protein: 12g, Carbohydrates: 50g, Fat: 12g, Fiber: 10g, Cholesterol: 15mg, Sodium: 500mg, Potassium: 700mg.

Fresh Tomato Salsa for Sweet Potato and Black Bean Breakfast Burrito

Ingredients:

- 1 cup barley
- 2 cups water
- 1 large apple, diced
- 1/2 cup fresh blueberries
- 1/2 cup fresh strawberries, sliced
- 1/4 cup chopped walnuts
- 2 tablespoons lemon juice
- 1 tablespoon honey
- 1/2 teaspoon cinnamon

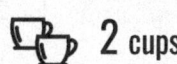 2 cups   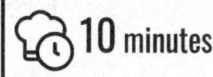 10 minutes    0 minutes

Directions:

1. Rinse barley under cold water. In a pot, bring barley and water to a boil. Reduce heat, cover, and simmer for 40 minutes.
2. Once barley is cooked, let it cool to room temperature.
3. Combine cooked barley, diced apple, blueberries, strawberries, and chopped walnuts in a large bowl.
4. Whisk together lemon juice, honey, and cinnamon in a small bowl.
5. Pour the dressing over the salad and toss to combine.
6. Serve the salad chilled or at room temperature.

This recipe offers a nutritious and refreshing low-cholesterol breakfast option that combines the hearty texture of barley with the sweetness of fresh fruits and the crunch of walnuts.

Nutritional Information: (per serving, approximate) Calories: 220, Protein: 5g, Carbohydrates: 45g, Fat: 4g, Fiber: 8g, Cholesterol: 0mg, Sodium: 10mg, Potassium: 280mg.

Brown Rice Tuna and Carrot Balls

Ingredients:

 4 servings    20 minutes   ~40 minutes

- 2 cups cooked brown rice (40 minutes approximate for cooking rice. Please refer to the packaging information for cooking time and method)
- 1 can (5 ounces) tuna in water, drained
- 1/2 cup grated carrot
- 2 tablespoons low-fat mayonnaise
- 1 tablespoon soy sauce
- Salt and pepper to taste
- Nori (seaweed) sheets, cut into strips (optional)

Directions:

1. Mix cooked rice, tuna, grated carrot, mayonnaise, and soy sauce in a bowl.
2. Season with salt and pepper to taste.
3. Wet your hands and form the mixture into small, round balls.
4. Wrap each ball with a strip of nori if using.
5. Serve immediately or refrigerate.

These Tuna-Carrot Rice Balls offer a unique and healthy low-cholesterol breakfast option, combining the wholesomeness of brown rice with the lean protein of tuna.

Nutritional Information: (per serving, approximate) Calories: 180, Protein: 10g, Carbohydrates: 25g, Fat: 4g, Fiber: 2g, Cholesterol: 15mg, Sodium: 300mg, Potassium: 200mg.

Baked Eggplant and Zucchini Casserole

Ingredients:

 4 servings   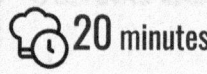 20 minutes   40 minutes

- 1 large eggplant, sliced
- 2 zucchinis, sliced
- 1 can (14.5 ounces) diced tomatoes, drained
- 1/2 cup low-fat mozzarella cheese, shredded
- 2 cloves garlic, minced
- 1 teaspoon dried basil
- 1 teaspoon dried oregano
- Salt and pepper to taste
- Olive oil spray

Directions:

1. Preheat oven to 375°F (190°C). Lightly spray a baking dish with olive oil.
2. Layer eggplant and zucchini slices in the dish, alternating each.
3. Sprinkle garlic, basil, oregano, salt, and pepper over the layers.
4. Spread the diced tomatoes evenly on top.
5. Cover with shredded mozzarella cheese.
6. Bake for 40 minutes or until vegetables are tender and cheese is bubbly.

This Baked Eggplant and Zucchini Casserole is a delicious and nutritious low-cholesterol dish, perfect for a healthy and satisfying breakfast.

Nutritional Information: (per serving, approximate) Calories: 150, Protein: 8g, Carbohydrates: 20g, Fat: 5g, Fiber: 6g, Cholesterol: 10mg, Sodium: 300mg, Potassium: 600mg.

Mango and Coconut Chia Pudding

 4 servings    15 minutes    2 hours

Ingredients:

- 1/4 cup chia seeds
- 1 cup coconut milk
- 1 ripe mango, diced
- 2 tablespoons honey or maple syrup
- 1/4 teaspoon vanilla extract

Directions:

1. Mix chia seeds, coconut milk, honey, and vanilla extract in a bowl.
2. Stir well and let sit for 5 minutes, then stir again to prevent clumping.
3. Cover and refrigerate for at least 2 hours or overnight.
4. Serve topped with diced mango.

This hearty multigrain porridge is a nutritious, low-cholesterol breakfast option, enriched with the goodness of dried fruits and nuts, perfect for a wholesome start to the day.

This tropical Mango and Coconut Chia Pudding is a delicious and nutritious low-cholesterol breakfast option, combining mango's sweetness with coconut milk's creaminess.

Blueberry and Lemon Ricotta Pancakes

 4 servings    10 minutes   15 minutes

Ingredients:

- 1 cup whole wheat flour
- 1/2 cup low-fat ricotta cheese
- 3/4 cup low-fat milk
- 1 egg
- 1 tablespoon lemon zest
- 1 cup blueberries
- 2 tablespoons honey or maple syrup
- 1 teaspoon baking powder
- Pinch of salt

Directions:

1. Mix flour, baking powder, and salt in a bowl.
2. Whisk ricotta, milk, egg, lemon zest, and honey in another bowl.
3. Combine wet and dry ingredients and gently fold in blueberries.
4. Heat a non-stick skillet over medium heat.
5. Pour 1/4 cup batter for each pancake, cook until bubbles form, then flip.
6. Serve warm.

These pancakes offer a delightful combination of blueberries and lemon, paired with the richness of ricotta, for a delicious low-cholesterol breakfast.

Nutritional Information: (per serving, approximate) Calories: 220, Protein: 10g, Carbohydrates: 35g, Fat: 5g, Fiber: 4g, Cholesterol: 55mg, Sodium: 200mg, Potassium: 200mg.

Mediterranean Chickpea and Avocado Salad

Ingredients:

 4 servings  15 minutes 0 minutes

- 1 can (15 ounces) chickpeas, drained and rinsed
- 1 ripe avocado, diced
- 1/2 cup cherry tomatoes, halved
- 1/4 cup red onion, finely chopped
- 1/4 cup cucumber, diced
- 2 tablespoons olive oil
- 1 tablespoon lemon juice
- 1/4 cup fresh parsley, chopped
- Salt and pepper to taste

Directions:

1. Combine chickpeas, avocado, cherry tomatoes, red onion, and cucumber in a large bowl.
2. Whisk together olive oil and lemon juice in a small bowl.
3. Pour dressing over the salad and gently toss.
4. Add parsley and season with salt and pepper.
5. Serve immediately or chill before serving.

This refreshing Mediterranean Chickpea and Avocado Salad is a perfect low-cholesterol breakfast option, offering a hearty blend of protein-rich chickpeas, healthy fats, and fresh vegetables.

Nutritional Information: (per serving, approximate) Calories: 250, Protein: 7g, Carbohydrates: 30g, Fat: 12g, Fiber: 8g, Cholesterol: 0mg, Sodium: 300mg, Potassium: 400mg.

Sun-dried Tomato and Spinach Omelet

 2 servings 5 minutes 5 minutes

Ingredients:

- 4 egg whites
- 1/4 cup sun-dried tomatoes, chopped
- 1 cup spinach, chopped
- Salt and pepper to taste
- Olive oil spray

Directions:

1. Whisk together egg whites with salt and pepper in a bowl.
2. Heat a non-stick skillet over medium heat and spray with olive oil.
3. Pour the egg whites into the skillet.
4. Add sun-dried tomatoes and spinach on top.
5. Cook until eggs are set and fold the omelet in half.

This Sun-dried Tomato and Spinach Omelet is a healthy, flavorful, low-cholesterol breakfast option, combining protein-rich egg whites with nutrient-dense vegetables.

Nutritional Information: (per serving, approximate) Calories: 100, Protein: 12g, Carbohydrates: 8g, Fat: 2g, Fiber: 2g, Cholesterol: 0mg, Sodium: 200mg, Potassium: 300mg.

Roasted Vegetable Breakfast Hash

Ingredients:

- 2 medium sweet potatoes, diced
- 1 red bell pepper, diced
- 1 zucchini, diced
- 1 onion, diced
- 2 tablespoons olive oil
- Salt and pepper to taste
- 1 teaspoon smoked paprika
- 4 egg whites

 4 servings   15 minutes   25 minutes

Directions:

1. Preheat the oven to 400°F (200°C). Toss sweet potatoes, bell pepper, zucchini, and onion with olive oil, salt, pepper, and smoked paprika.
2. Spread vegetables on a baking sheet and roast for 25 minutes, stirring halfway through.
3. In the last 5 minutes of roasting, create four wells in the vegetables and carefully pour an egg white into each well.
4. Return to the oven and cook until egg whites are set.

This Roasted Vegetable Breakfast Hash offers a nutritious and satisfying start to the day, featuring a colorful mix of vegetables topped with protein-rich egg whites.

Nutritional Information: (per serving, approximate) Calories: 200, Protein: 6g, Carbohydrates: 30g, Fat: 7g, Fiber: 5g, Cholesterol: 0mg, Sodium: 200mg, Potassium: 500mg.

Whole Grain Garlic Herb Bread

Ingredients:

- 4 slices of whole-grain bread
- 2 tablespoons olive oil
- 2 garlic cloves, minced
- 1 teaspoon dried rosemary
- 1 teaspoon dried thyme
- Salt and pepper to taste

 4 servings   10 minutes   10 minutes

Directions:

1. Preheat your oven to 350°F (180°C).
2. In a small bowl, combine the olive oil, minced garlic, dried rosemary, thyme, salt, and pepper.
3. Brush both sides of the bread slices with the prepared mixture.
4. Place the bread on a baking sheet and bake for about 10 minutes until the bread is crispy and golden.
5. Remove from the oven, let cool slightly, and serve.

This Whole Grain Garlic Herb Bread is a heart-healthy side that complements any meal, offering a delicious way to enjoy the benefits of whole grains along with the aromatic flavors of garlic and herbs, perfect for a low-cholesterol diet.

Nutritional Information (per serving, approximate): Calories: 150, Protein: 4g, Carbohydrates: 18g, Fat: 7g, Fiber: 3g, Cholesterol: 0mg, Sodium: 200mg, Potassium: 100mg.

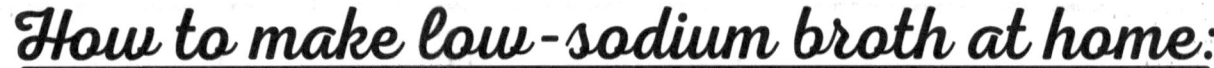

How to make low-sodium broth at home:

- To make a broth with low sodium content for a cholesterol-friendly diet, follow these tips:

- Use Fresh Ingredients: Make broth using fresh vegetables, such as onions, carrots, celery, and herbs like thyme or parsley. For lower cholesterol, you can add chicken or turkey, preferably skinless and boneless.

- Avoid Salt: Do not add salt or use very minimal amounts. You can enhance flavors with herbs and spices instead.
- Skim Fat: If using meat, let the broth cool and skim off the fat that rises to the top.

- Homemade is Best: Store-bought broths often contain high sodium levels, even the "low sodium" versions. Homemade allows you to control the sodium content.

- By following these steps, you can create a flavorful broth that aligns with low-sodium and low-cholesterol dietary guidelines.

Lentil and Spinach Soup

  4 servings   10 minutes   30 minutes

Ingredients:

- 1 cup dried lentils, rinsed
- 4 cups low-sodium vegetable broth
- 1 onion, diced
- 2 cloves garlic, minced
- 2 carrots, diced
- 1 teaspoon ground cumin
- 1/2 teaspoon paprika
- 3 cups fresh spinach leaves
- Salt and pepper to taste
- 1 tablespoon olive oil

Directions:

1. Heat olive oil in a large pot. Sauté onion and garlic until translucent.
2. Add carrots, cumin, and paprika, and cook for 2 minutes.
3. Add lentils and vegetable broth. Bring to a boil, then reduce heat and simmer for 20 minutes.
4. Stir in spinach and cook until wilted.
5. Season with salt and pepper.
6. Serve hot.

This Lentil and Spinach Soup is a hearty and nutritious low-cholesterol option, perfect for a healthy and satisfying meal.

Nutritional Information: (per serving, approximate) Calories: 220, Protein: 12g, Carbohydrates: 35g, Fat: 4g, Fiber: 15g, Cholesterol: 0mg, Sodium: 300mg, Potassium: 700mg.

Hearty Vegetable Stew

Ingredients:

 4 servings   15 minutes   35 minutes

- 1 onion, chopped
- 2 carrots, diced
- 2 celery stalks, diced
- 1 bell pepper, chopped
- 2 potatoes, diced
- 1 zucchini, chopped
- 1 can (14.5 ounces) diced tomatoes
- 4 cups low-sodium vegetable broth
- 2 teaspoons dried thyme
- Salt and pepper to taste
- 2 tablespoons olive oil

Directions:

1. Heat olive oil in a large pot. Sauté onion, carrots, and celery until softened.
2. Add bell pepper, potatoes, and zucchini, and cook for 5 minutes.
3. Stir in diced tomatoes, vegetable broth, and thyme.
4. Bring to a boil, then reduce heat and simmer for 30 minutes.
5. Season with salt and pepper.
6. Serve hot.

This Hearty Vegetable Stew is a warming and nutritious low-cholesterol meal, perfect for a cozy and healthy dinner.

Nutritional Information: (per serving, approximate) Calories: 200, Protein: 5g, Carbohydrates: 35g, Fat: 5g, Fiber: 6g, Cholesterol: 0mg, Sodium: 300mg, Potassium: 800mg.

Tomato Basil Soup

Ingredients:

 4 servings   10 minutes   30 minutes

- 4 cups diced tomatoes (fresh or canned)
- 1 onion, chopped
- 2 cloves garlic, minced
- 4 cups low-sodium vegetable broth
- 1/4 cup fresh basil, chopped
- Salt and pepper to taste
- 1 tablespoon olive oil

Directions:

1. Heat olive oil in a pot. Sauté onion and garlic until translucent.
2. Add tomatoes and cook for 5 minutes.
3. Pour in vegetable broth and bring to a boil.
4. Simmer for 20 minutes.
5. Add basil, and use an immersion blender to puree the soup until smooth.
6. Season with salt and pepper.

This Tomato Basil Soup is a classic and tasty low-cholesterol dish, perfect for any meal.

Nutritional Information: (per serving, approximate) Calories: 100, Protein: 2g, Carbohydrates: 15g, Fat: 4g, Fiber: 3g, Cholesterol: 0mg, Sodium: 200mg, Potassium: 400mg.

Mushroom Barley Soup

Ingredients:

 4 servings    15 minutes   40 minutes

- 1 cup pearl barley
- 4 cups sliced mushrooms
- 1 onion, chopped
- 2 cloves garlic, minced
- 6 cups low-sodium vegetable broth
- 1 carrot, diced
- 1 teaspoon dried thyme
- Salt and pepper to taste
- 2 tablespoons olive oil

Directions:

1. Heat olive oil in a large pot. Sauté onion, garlic, and mushrooms until softened.
2. Add barley, carrot, thyme, and vegetable broth.
3. Bring to a boil, then reduce heat and simmer for 30-40 minutes.
4. Season with salt and pepper.

This hearty Mushroom Barley Soup is a flavorful and nutritious low-cholesterol option, perfect for a comforting and satisfying meal.

Nutritional Information: (per serving, approximate) Calories: 250, Protein: 8g, Carbohydrates: 45g, Fat: 5g, Fiber: 10g, Cholesterol: 0mg, Sodium: 200mg, Potassium: 500mg.

Minestrone with Whole-Grain Pasta

Ingredients:

 4 servings   15 minutes   30 minutes

- 1 cup whole-grain pasta
- 1 onion, chopped
- 2 cloves garlic, minced
- 1 carrot, diced
- 1 zucchini, diced
- 1 can (14.5 ounces) diced tomatoes
- 4 cups low-sodium vegetable broth
- 1 can (15 ounces) kidney beans, drained and rinsed
- 1 teaspoon dried basil
- Salt and pepper to taste
- 2 tablespoons olive oil

Directions:

1. Cook pasta according to package instructions; set aside.
2. In a pot, heat olive oil. Sauté onion and garlic.
3. Add carrot, zucchini, tomatoes, broth, beans, and basil.
4. Bring to a boil, then simmer for 20 minutes.
5. Stir in cooked pasta.
6. Season with salt and pepper.

This hearty Minestrone with Whole-Grain Pasta is a nutritious and filling low-cholesterol meal, perfect for any day.

Nutritional Information: (per serving, approximate) Calories: 260, Protein: 10g, Carbohydrates: 45g, Fat: 6g, Fiber: 8g, Cholesterol: 0mg, Sodium: 300mg, Potassium: 600mg.

Eggplant and Lentil Stew

Ingredients:

 4 servings   15 minutes   40 minutes

- 1 cup dried lentils, rinsed
- 1 large eggplant, diced
- 1 onion, chopped
- 2 cloves garlic, minced
- 1 can (14.5 ounces) diced tomatoes
- 4 cups low-sodium vegetable broth
- 1 teaspoon paprika
- 1 teaspoon cumin
- Salt and pepper to taste
- 2 tablespoons olive oil

Directions:

1. Heat olive oil in a pot. Sauté onion and garlic until softened.
2. Add eggplant, lentils, tomatoes, paprika, cumin, and vegetable broth.
3. Bring to a boil, then reduce heat and simmer for 35-40 minutes.
4. Season with salt and pepper.

This Eggplant and Lentil Stew is a hearty, low-cholesterol meal rich in plant-based protein and fiber.

Nutritional Information: (per serving, approximate) Calories: 250, Protein: 12g, Carbohydrates: 35g, Fat: 7g, Fiber: 15g, Cholesterol: 0mg, Sodium: 200mg, Potassium: 700mg.

Chicken and Vegetable Soup

 4 servings   15 minutes   30 minutes

Ingredients:

- 2 chicken breasts, skinless and boneless
- 4 cups low-sodium chicken broth
- 1 onion, chopped
- 2 carrots, sliced
- 2 celery stalks, sliced
- 1 cup green beans, trimmed
- Salt and pepper to taste
- 1 teaspoon dried thyme
- 1 tablespoon olive oil

Directions:

1. In a pot, heat olive oil. Cook chicken until no longer pink, then set aside.
2. Sauté onion, carrots, and celery in the same pot.
3. Add chicken broth, green beans, thyme, and cooked chicken.
4. Simmer for 20 minutes.
5. Season with salt and pepper.

This Chicken and Vegetable Soup is a healthy, low-cholesterol option, providing a comforting and nutritious meal.

Nutritional Information: (per serving, approximate) Calories: 180, Protein: 22g, Carbohydrates: 10g, Fat: 6g, Fiber: 3g, Cholesterol: 50mg, Sodium: 200mg, Potassium: 400mg.

Lean Beef and Vegetable Soup

Ingredients:

 4 servings   15 minutes   45 minutes

- 1 lb lean beef, cut into small cubes
- 4 cups low-sodium beef broth
- 1 onion, chopped
- 2 carrots, sliced
- 2 celery stalks, sliced
- 1 cup green beans, trimmed
- 1 can (14.5 ounces) diced tomatoes
- Salt and pepper to taste
- 1 teaspoon dried thyme
- 1 tablespoon olive oil

Directions:

1. Heat olive oil in a pot. Brown the beef cubes, then set aside.
2. Sauté onion, carrots, and celery.
3. Add beef broth, tomatoes, thyme, and browned beef.
4. Simmer for 30-40 minutes.
5. Add green beans and cook for an additional 5 minutes.
6. Season with salt and pepper.

This Lean Beef and Vegetable Soup is a hearty and healthy low-cholesterol meal, perfect for a nutritious and satisfying dish.

Nutritional Information: (per serving, approximate) Calories: 250, Protein: 26g, Carbohydrates: 15g, Fat: 9g, Fiber: 4g, Cholesterol: 50mg, Sodium: 200mg, Potassium: 700mg.

Turkey and Barley Stew

 4 servings   15 minutes   40 minutes

Ingredients:

- 1 lb lean ground turkey
- 1 cup pearl barley
- 1 onion, chopped
- 2 carrots, diced
- 2 celery stalks, diced
- 4 cups low-sodium chicken broth
- 1 can (14.5 ounces) diced tomatoes
- 1 teaspoon dried thyme
- Salt and pepper to taste
- 2 tablespoons olive oil

Directions:

1. Brown the ground turkey in olive oil and set aside.
2. Sauté onion, carrots, and celery in the same pot.
3. Add barley, chicken broth, tomatoes, thyme, and cooked turkey.
4. Bring to a boil, then reduce heat and simmer for 30 minutes.
5. Season with salt and pepper.

This wholesome Turkey and Barley Stew is a nutritious low-cholesterol meal, perfect for a comforting and hearty dish.

Nutritional Information: (per serving, approximate) Calories: 300, Protein: 22g, Carbohydrates: 35g, Fat: 9g, Fiber: 8g, Cholesterol: 50mg, Sodium: 200mg, Potassium: 600mg.

Chicken and Lentil Soup

Ingredients:

- 1 lb chicken breast, skinless and boneless
- 1 cup dried lentils, rinsed
- 1 onion, chopped
- 2 carrots, sliced
- 2 celery stalks, sliced
- 4 cups low-sodium chicken broth
- 1 teaspoon dried thyme
- Salt and pepper to taste
- 2 tablespoons olive oil

 4 servings   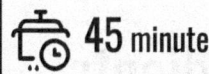 15 minutes   45 minutes

Directions:

1. Cut chicken into small pieces. Heat olive oil in a pot and cook chicken until no longer pink.
2. Add onion, carrots, and celery. Cook until softened.
3. Add lentils, chicken broth, and thyme.
4. Bring to a boil, then simmer for 30-35 minutes.
5. Season with salt and pepper.

This Chicken and Lentil Soup is a hearty, nutritious low-cholesterol meal, ideal for a satisfying and healthy diet.

Nutritional Information: (per serving, approximate) Calories: 300, Protein: 28g, Carbohydrates: 30g, Fat: 8g, Fiber: 10g, Cholesterol: 60mg, Sodium: 200mg, Potassium: 700mg.

Mediterranean Fish Soup

Ingredients:

- 1 lb white fish fillets (such as cod or tilapia)
- 1 onion, chopped
- 2 cloves garlic, minced
- 1 bell pepper, chopped
- 1 can (14.5 ounces) diced tomatoes
- 4 cups low-sodium vegetable broth
- 1 teaspoon dried oregano
- Salt and pepper to taste
- 2 tablespoons olive oil
- Fresh parsley for garnish

 2 servings   10 minutes   0 minutes

Directions:

1. Heat olive oil in a pot and sauté onion, garlic, and bell pepper.
2. Add tomatoes, vegetable broth, and oregano, and boil.
3. Add fish fillets and simmer for 20 minutes.
4. Season with salt and pepper.
5. Garnish with fresh parsley before serving.

This Mediterranean Fish Soup is a flavorful and heart-healthy meal, perfect for a low-cholesterol diet.

Nutritional Information: (per serving, approximate) Calories: 200, Protein: 22g, Carbohydrates: 10g, Fat: 8g, Fiber: 2g, Cholesterol: 50mg, Sodium: 300mg, Potassium: 500mg.

Shrimp and Vegetable Miso Soup

Ingredients:

 4 servings 10 minutes 15 minutes

- 1/2 lb shrimp, peeled and deveined
- 4 cups water
- 2 tablespoons miso paste
- 1 cup mushrooms, sliced
- 1 cup bok choy, chopped
- 1 carrot, sliced
- 1 green onion, chopped
- 1 teaspoon ginger, grated
- 1 tablespoon low-sodium soy sauce

Directions:

1. Boil water, then simmer with ginger and soy sauce.
2. Add vegetables and cook until tender.
3. Add shrimp and cook until pink.
4. Dissolve miso in a separate bowl with soup broth and add back.
5. Serve hot with green onion.

This Shrimp and Vegetable Miso Soup is a heart-healthy, low-cholesterol meal, combining lean protein and nutritious vegetables.

Nutritional Information: (per serving, approximate) Calories: 100, Protein: 12g, Carbs: 8g, Fat: 2g, Fiber: 2g, Cholesterol: 85mg, Sodium: 400mg, Potassium: 300mg.

Cod and Potato Chowder

Ingredients:

  4 servings 15 minutes 30 minutes

- 1 lb cod fillets, cut into chunks
- 2 large potatoes, peeled and diced
- 1 onion, chopped
- 2 carrots, sliced
- 2 celery stalks, sliced
- 4 cups low-sodium vegetable broth
- 1 cup low-fat milk
- 2 tablespoons flour
- 1 tablespoon olive oil
- Salt and pepper to taste
- Fresh parsley for garnish

Directions:

1. Heat olive oil in a pot. Sauté onion, carrots, and celery.
2. Add potatoes and vegetable broth. Simmer until potatoes are tender.
3. Whisk milk and flour until smooth in a bowl, then add to the pot.
4. Add cod and cook until fish is opaque and flakes easily.
5. Season with salt and pepper.
6. Garnish with parsley before serving.

This Cod and Potato Chowder is a comforting, nutritious, low-cholesterol meal, perfect for a hearty and healthy diet.

Nutritional Information: (per serving, approximate) Calories: 250, Protein: 25g, Carbohydrates: 30g, Fat: 5g, Fiber: 4g, Cholesterol: 45mg, Sodium: 200mg, Potassium: 800mg.

Spicy Tomato Seafood Soup

Ingredients:

 4 servings  15 minutes 25 minutes

- 1 lb mixed seafood (shrimp, scallops, squid)
- 1 can (14.5 ounces) diced tomatoes
- 4 cups low-sodium vegetable broth
- 1 onion, chopped
- 2 cloves garlic, minced
- 1 red bell pepper, diced
- 1 teaspoon red pepper flakes (adjust to taste)
- 1 teaspoon paprika
- Salt and pepper to taste
- 2 tablespoons olive oil
- Fresh parsley for garnish

Directions:

1. Heat olive oil in a pot. Sauté onion, garlic, and bell pepper.
2. Add diced tomatoes, vegetable broth, red pepper flakes, and paprika.
3. Bring to a boil, then simmer for 15 minutes.
4. Add seafood and cook until done (shrimp should be pink, scallops firm).
5. Season with salt and pepper.
6. Garnish with parsley before serving.

YOU CAN EXCLUDE RED PEPPERS IF YOU HAVE AN INDIVIDUAL CONTRAINDICATIONS.S

This Spicy Tomato Seafood Soup is a flavorful and heart-healthy dish, perfect for a low-cholesterol diet. Combining seafood and spicy tomato broth creates a delicious and satisfying meal.

Nutritional Information: (per serving, approximate) Calories: 200, Protein: 20g, Carbohydrates: 15g, Fat: 7g, Fiber: 3g, Cholesterol: 85mg, Sodium: 300mg, Potassium: 500mg.

Salmon and Asparagus Soup

Ingredients:

 4 servings  10 minutes  20 minutes

- 1 lb salmon fillet, skin removed and cut into cubes
- 1 bunch asparagus, trimmed and cut into 1-inch pieces
- 4 cups low-sodium vegetable broth
- 1 onion, chopped
- 2 cloves garlic, minced
- 1 lemon, juice and zest
- Salt and pepper to taste
- 2 tablespoons olive oil
- Fresh dill for garnish

Directions:

1. Heat olive oil in a pot. Sauté onion and garlic until translucent.
2. Add vegetable broth and bring to a boil.
3. Reduce heat, add asparagus, and simmer for 10 minutes.
4. Add salmon cubes and cook for 5-7 minutes until the salmon is cooked.
5. Stir in lemon juice and zest. Season with salt and pepper.
6. Serve hot, garnished with fresh dill.

This Salmon and Asparagus Soup is a light and healthy low-cholesterol meal, rich in omega-3 fatty acids and essential nutrients, perfect for a heart-healthy diet.

Nutritional Information: (per serving, approximate) Calories: 250, Protein: 25g, Carbohydrates: 8g, Fat: 13g, Fiber: 2g, Cholesterol: 60mg, Sodium: 200mg, Potassium: 650mg.

Quinoa Tabbouleh

 4 servings |  15 minutes | 15 minutes

Ingredients:

- 1 cup quinoa, rinsed
- 2 cups water
- 1 cucumber, diced
- 2 tomatoes, diced
- 1/4 cup fresh parsley, chopped
- 1/4 cup fresh mint, chopped (optional)
- 3 tablespoons olive oil
- Juice of 1 lemon
- Salt and pepper to taste

Directions:

1. In a saucepan, bring water to a boil. Add quinoa and reduce to a simmer. Cook for 15 minutes or until water is absorbed. Let cool.
2. In a large bowl, combine cooled quinoa, cucumber, tomatoes, parsley, and mint (if using).
3. Whisk together olive oil and lemon juice in a small bowl.
4. Pour the dressing over the quinoa mixture and toss to combine.
5. Season with salt and pepper.
6. Serve chilled or at room temperature.

This Quinoa Tabbouleh, with the optional addition of fresh mint, is a versatile and low-cholesterol side dish, offering a refreshing and nutritious complement to any meal.

Nutritional Information: (per serving, approximate) Calories: 220, Protein: 6g, Carbohydrates: 30g, Fat: 9g, Fiber: 5g, Cholesterol: 0mg, Sodium: 10mg, Potassium: 400mg.

Steamed Broccoli with Lemon Zest

 4 servings |  5 minutes |  5 minutes

Ingredients:

- 4 cups broccoli florets
- Zest of 1 lemon
- 1 tablespoon olive oil
- Salt and pepper to taste

Directions:

1. In a steamer, steam broccoli florets for about 5 minutes or until they are bright green and tender.
2. Transfer the steamed broccoli to a serving dish.
3. Drizzle olive oil over the broccoli.
4. Sprinkle lemon zest, salt, and pepper over the broccoli.
5. Toss gently to coat the broccoli with the seasoning.
6. Serve warm.

This Steamed Broccoli with Lemon Zest is a light, healthy, low-cholesterol side dish, perfect for adding a fresh and flavorful touch to any meal.

Nutritional Information: (per serving, approximate) Calories: 70, Protein: 3g, Carbohydrates: 7g, Fat: 4g, Fiber: 2g, Cholesterol: 0mg, Sodium: 30mg, Potassium: 230mg.

Whole-Grain Brown Rice Pilaf

Ingredients:

  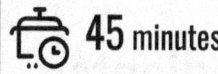

4 servings   **10 minutes**   **45 minutes**

- 1 cup whole-grain brown rice
- 2 cups low-sodium vegetable broth
- 1 onion, chopped
- 1 carrot, diced
- 1/2 cup peas
- 1/2 teaspoon dried thyme
- 1 tablespoon olive oil
- Salt and pepper to taste

Directions:

1. Heat olive oil in a saucepan over medium heat. Sauté onion and carrot until softened.
2. Add brown rice and stir for a few minutes until lightly toasted.
3. Pour in vegetable broth and bring to a boil.
4. Reduce heat to low, cover, and simmer for 40-45 minutes or until the rice is tender and liquid is absorbed.
5. Stir in peas and thyme. Cook for an additional 5 minutes.
6. Season with salt and pepper.
7. Serve warm.

This Whole-Grain Brown Rice Pilaf is a nutritious and satisfying low-cholesterol side dish, perfect for complementing a variety of main courses.

Nutritional Information: (per serving, approximate) Calories: 220, Protein: 5g, Carbohydrates: 40g, Fat: 5g, Fiber: 4g, Cholesterol: 0mg, Sodium: 150mg, Potassium: 250mg.

Sautéed Spinach with Garlic

Ingredients:

4 servings   **5 minutes**   **5 minutes**

- 4 cups fresh spinach leaves
- 2 cloves garlic, minced
- 1 tablespoon olive oil
- Salt and pepper to taste

Directions:

1. Heat olive oil in a large skillet over medium heat.
2. Add minced garlic and sauté for about 30 seconds, until fragrant.
3. Add spinach leaves to the skillet and saute for 2-3 minutes or until spinach is wilted.
4. Season with salt and pepper.
5. Serve immediately.

This Sautéed Spinach with Garlic is a simple, healthy, and flavorful low-cholesterol side dish that pairs well with various main courses.

Nutritional Information: (per serving, approximate) Calories: 50, Protein: 2g, Carbohydrates: 4g, Fat: 3g, Fiber: 2g, Cholesterol: 0mg, Sodium: 50mg, Potassium: 300mg.

Cauliflower Mash

 4 servings | 10 minutes | 15 minutes

Ingredients:

- 1 large head of cauliflower, cut into florets
- 2 cloves garlic, minced
- 1 tablespoon olive oil
- Salt and pepper to taste
- Optional: 1-2 tablespoons low-fat milk or almond milk for creaminess

Directions:

1. Steam the cauliflower florets until very tender, about 15 minutes.
2. In a skillet, heat olive oil and lightly sauté minced garlic until fragrant.
3. Transfer steamed cauliflower and sautéed garlic to a food processor.
4. Blend until smooth. If needed, add a little milk for desired consistency.
5. Season with salt and pepper to taste.
6. Serve warm as a side dish.

This Cauliflower Mash is a delicious and healthy low-cholesterol alternative to traditional mashed potatoes, offering a similar texture and taste with fewer carbs and calories.

Nutritional Information: (per serving, approximate) Calories: 70, Protein: 3g, Carbohydrates: 10g, Fat: 3g, Fiber: 4g, Cholesterol: 0mg, Sodium: 50mg, Potassium: 450mg.

Grilled Asparagus with Balsamic Glaze

 4 servings | 10 minutes | 10 minutes

Ingredients:

- 1 lb fresh asparagus, trimmed
- 2 tablespoons olive oil
- Salt and pepper to taste
- 2 tablespoons balsamic vinegar
- Optional: 1 teaspoon honey or maple syrup (for a touch of sweetness)

Directions:

1. Preheat the grill to medium-high heat.
2. Toss asparagus with olive oil, salt, and pepper.
3. Grill asparagus for about 10 minutes, turning occasionally, until tender and slightly charred.
4. In a small saucepan, heat balsamic vinegar (and honey or maple syrup if using) over low heat until slightly thickened, about 3-5 minutes.
5. Drizzle balsamic glaze over grilled asparagus.
6. Serve warm as a side dish.

This Grilled Asparagus with Balsamic Glaze is a flavorful and elegant low-cholesterol side dish that is perfect for enhancing any meal with its savory and slightly sweet notes.

Nutritional Information: (per serving, approximate) Calories: 80, Protein: 3g, Carbohydrates: 7g, Fat: 5g, Fiber: 2g, Cholesterol: 0mg, Sodium: 10mg, Potassium: 230mg.

Roasted Brussels Sprouts with Lemon

Ingredients:

- 1 lb Brussels sprouts, trimmed and halved
- 2 tablespoons olive oil
- Juice of 1 lemon
- Zest of 1 lemon
- Salt and pepper to taste

 **4** servings  **10** minutes  **20** minutes

Directions:

1. Preheat the oven to 400°F (200°C).
2. Toss Brussels sprouts with olive oil, salt, and pepper in a mixing bowl.
3. Spread them out on a baking sheet in a single layer.
4. Roast in the oven for 20 minutes or until tender and edges are crispy.
5. Remove from the oven and transfer to a serving bowl.
6. Drizzle with fresh lemon juice and sprinkle lemon zest over the top.
7. Serve warm as a side dish.

This Roasted Brussels Sprouts with Lemon is a simple, healthy, and delicious low-cholesterol side dish that brings a bright and tangy flavor to the sprouts.

Nutritional Information: (per serving, approximate) Calories: 100, Protein: 4g, Carbohydrates: 10g, Fat: 6g, Fiber: 4g, Cholesterol: 0mg, Sodium: 25mg, Potassium: 350mg.

Barley and Roasted Vegetable Pilaf

 **4** servings **15** minutes **40** minutes

Ingredients:

- 1 cup pearl barley
- 2 cups low-sodium vegetable broth
- 1 zucchini, diced
- 1 red bell pepper, diced
- 1 yellow bell pepper, diced
- 1 onion, diced
- 2 cloves garlic, minced
- 2 tablespoons olive oil
- Salt and pepper to taste
- Fresh parsley, chopped (for garnish)

Directions:

1. Preheat oven to 400°F (200°C). Toss zucchini, bell peppers, onion, and garlic with one tablespoon of olive oil, salt, and pepper. Spread on a baking sheet and roast for 20-25 minutes.
2. While vegetables are roasting, rinse barley under cold water.
3. In a saucepan, bring vegetable broth to a boil. Add barley, reduce heat to low, cover, and simmer for 30-40 minutes until tender and liquid is absorbed.
4. Combine cooked barley with roasted vegetables. Adjust seasoning with salt and pepper.
5. Drizzle with the remaining one tablespoon of olive oil.
6. Garnish with fresh parsley before serving.

This Barley and Roasted Vegetable Pilaf is a nutritious and flavorful low-cholesterol side dish.

Nutritional Information: (per serving, approximate) Calories: 220, Protein: 6g, Carbohydrates: 40g, Fat: 6g, Fiber: 9g, Cholesterol: 0mg, Sodium: 50mg, Potassium: 300mg.

Whole Wheat Couscous with Herbs and Lemon

 **4 servings** **5 minutes** **10 minutes**

Ingredients:

- 1 cup whole wheat couscous
- 1 1/4 cups low-sodium vegetable broth
- Juice of 1/2 lemon
- 1/4 cup fresh parsley, chopped
- 1/4 cup fresh mint, chopped (optional)
- 2 tablespoons olive oil
- Salt and pepper to taste

Directions:

- In a saucepan, bring the vegetable broth to a boil.
- Add the whole wheat couscous to the boiling broth, then remove from heat and cover. Let it stand for 5 minutes.
- Fluff the couscous with a fork to separate the grains.
- Stir in lemon juice, chopped parsley, chopped mint, and olive oil.
- Season with salt and pepper to taste.
- Serve warm or at room temperature as a side dish.

This Whole Wheat Couscous with Herbs and Lemon is a light, flavorful, and heart-healthy side dish, perfect for a low-cholesterol diet. The combination of fresh herbs and lemon brings a delightful freshness to the dish.

Nutritional Information: (per serving, approximate) Calories: 230, Protein: 7g, Carbohydrates: 40g, Fat: 6g, Fiber: 6g, Cholesterol: 0mg, Sodium: 50mg, Potassium: 200mg.

Bulgur Wheat with Grilled Zucchini and Peppers

 **4 servings**  **15 minutes**  **20 minutes**

Ingredients:

- 1 cup bulgur wheat
- 2 cups water
- 1 zucchini, sliced
- 1 red bell pepper, sliced
- 1 yellow bell pepper, sliced
- 2 tablespoons olive oil
- Salt and pepper to taste
- Fresh parsley, chopped (for garnish)

Directions:

1. In a saucepan, bring water to a boil. Add the bulgur wheat, reduce heat to low, cover, and simmer for 12-15 minutes or until water is absorbed. Fluff with a fork.
2. Preheat the grill to medium-high heat. Brush zucchini and bell peppers with 1 tablespoon olive oil and season with salt and pepper.
3. Grill zucchini and peppers for about 3-4 minutes per side or until they have grill marks and are tender.
4. Chop grilled vegetables into bite-sized pieces.
5. Combine cooked bulgur wheat with grilled vegetables in a large bowl. Drizzle with remaining olive oil.
6. Garnish with fresh parsley.
7. Serve warm as a nutritious side dish.

This Bulgur Wheat with Grilled Zucchini and Peppers is a wholesome and flavorful low-cholesterol side dish, perfect for adding a delicious and nutritious element to any meal.

Nutritional Information: (per serving, approximate) Calories: 220, Protein: 6g, Carbohydrates: 35g, Fat: 7g, Fiber: 8g, Cholesterol: 0mg, Sodium: 10mg, Potassium: 300mg.

Wild Rice with Cranberries and Almonds

Ingredients:

- 1 cup wild rice
- 3 cups water
- 1/2 cup dried cranberries
- 1/2 cup slivered almonds, toasted
- 2 tablespoons olive oil
- Salt and pepper to taste
- Fresh parsley, chopped (for garnish)

This Wild Rice with Cranberries and Almonds is a festive and flavorful low-cholesterol side dish, combining nutty wild rice with sweet cranberries and crunchy almonds. It's perfect for a healthy and delicious meal accompaniment.

 4 servings  10 minutes  45 minutes

Directions:

1. Rinse wild rice under cold water.
2. Bring 3 cups of water to a boil in a saucepan. Add wild rice, reduce heat to low, cover, and simmer for 40-45 minutes until the rice is tender and most water is absorbed.
3. Drain any excess water and let the rice cool slightly.
4. In a large bowl, mix the cooked wild rice with dried cranberries and toasted almonds
5. Drizzle with olive oil and season with salt and pepper. Toss well to combine.
6. Garnish with fresh parsley before serving.
7. Serve warm or at room temperature as a side dish.

Nutritional Information: (per serving, approximate) Calories: 280, Protein: 7g, Carbohydrates: 40g, Fat: 12g, Fiber: 4g, Cholesterol: 0mg, Sodium: 10mg, Potassium: 250mg.

Garlic and Herb Roasted Potatoes

Ingredients:

- 1.5 pounds small red or yellow potatoes, halved or quartered if large
- 2 tablespoons olive oil
- 3 cloves garlic, minced
- 1 teaspoon dried rosemary
- 1 teaspoon dried thyme
- 1/2 teaspoon dried oregano
- Salt and pepper to taste
- Fresh parsley, chopped (for garnish)

These potatoes offer a satisfying texture With a crisp exterior and soft, fluffy interior. They are seasoned with a fragrant blend of herbs and garlic, making them a perfect heart-healthy side dish for any meal.

 4 servings 10 minutes  30 minutes

Directions:

1. Preheat your oven to 400°F (200°C). Line a large baking sheet with parchment paper for easy cleanup.
2. In a large bowl, toss the potatoes with olive oil, minced garlic, dried rosemary, thyme, oregano, salt, and pepper until the potatoes are well coated.
3. Spread the potatoes in a single layer on the prepared baking sheet, ensuring they have space between them for even roasting.
4. Roast in the preheated oven for about 30 minutes until the potatoes are golden brown and tender when pierced with a fork. Halfway through the cooking time, use a spatula to flip the potatoes for even browning.
5. Once roasted, remove the potatoes from the oven and taste to adjust the seasoning with additional salt and pepper if needed.
6. Transfer the roasted potatoes to a serving dish and sprinkle with fresh chopped parsley for garnish.
7. Serve the Garlic and Herb Roasted Potatoes as a flavorful and healthy side dish alongside your Herb-Crusted Halibut with Roasted Vegetables.

Nutritional Information (per serving, approximate): Calories: 200, Protein: 4 g, Carbohydrates: 35 g, Fat: 5 g, Fiber: 4 g, Cholesterol: 0 mg, Sodium: 75 mg, Potassium: 800 mg

Mushroom and Barley Risotto

 4 servings  15 minutes  45 minutes

Ingredients:

- 1 cup pearled barley, rinsed
- 4 cups low-sodium vegetable broth
- 2 tablespoons olive oil
- 1 small onion, finely chopped
- 2 cloves garlic, minced
- 1 pound assorted mushrooms (e.g., cremini, shiitake, button), sliced
- 1/2 cup dry white wine (optional)
- 1/4 cup grated Parmesan cheese (optional for vegan version)
- 2 tablespoons fresh parsley, chopped
- Salt and pepper to taste

Directions:

1. Heat 1 tablespoon of olive oil in a large saucepan over medium heat. Add the onion and garlic, and cook until soft and translucent, for about 5 minutes.
2. Add the mushrooms to the saucepan, cooking until they have released their moisture and are golden brown, about 8 minutes.
3. Stir in the barley and cook for 1-2 minutes to lightly toast it, then add the wine (if using) and cook until it has evaporated.
4. Gradually add the vegetable broth, stirring frequently, one cup at a time. Allow each addition to be absorbed before adding the next. Continue until the barley is tender and creamy, about 30-40 minutes.
5. Remove from heat and stir in the Parmesan cheese (or nutritional yeast) and fresh parsley. Season with salt and pepper to taste.
6. Serve warm, drizzling with the remaining olive oil if desired.

This Mushroom and Barley Risotto combines the earthy flavors of assorted mushrooms with the chewy, satisfying texture of barley for a hearty, comforting meal. Perfect for a cozy evening, it's a nutritious twist on the classic risotto that's rich in flavor and beneficial for maintaining a low-cholesterol diet.

Nutritional Information (per serving, approximate): Calories: 350, Protein: 10g, Carbohydrates: 55g, Fat: 9g, Fiber: 10g, Cholesterol: 5mg (without Parmesan cheese: 0mg), Sodium: 200mg, Potassium: 400mg.

Baked Cod with Tomato and Basil

Ingredients:

- 4 cod fillets (about 6 ounces each)
- 2 cups cherry tomatoes, halved
- 1/4 cup fresh basil leaves, chopped
- 2 cloves garlic, minced
- 2 tablespoons olive oil
- Salt and pepper to taste
- Lemon wedges for serving

 4 servings | 10 minutes | 20 minutes

Directions:

1. Preheat the oven to 400°F (200°C).
2. Arrange the cod fillets in a single layer in a baking dish.
3. Mix cherry tomatoes, basil, garlic, olive oil, salt, and pepper in a bowl.
4. Spoon the tomato mixture over the cod fillets.
5. Bake in the oven for 20 minutes or until the fish flakes easily with a fork.
6. Serve hot, garnished with lemon wedges.

This Baked Cod with Tomato and Basil is a delicious and heart-healthy main dish, perfect for a low-cholesterol diet. The combination of tender cod, juicy tomatoes, and fresh basil creates a flavorful and satisfying meal.

Nutritional Information: (per serving, approximate) Calories: 200, Protein: 25g, Carbohydrates: 6g, Fat: 8g, Fiber: 2g, Cholesterol: 60mg, Sodium: 100mg, Potassium: 600mg.

Shrimp Stir-Fry with Vegetables

Ingredients:

- 1 lb shrimp, peeled and deveined
- 2 cups broccoli florets
- 1 red bell pepper, sliced
- 1 carrot, sliced
- 1 zucchini, sliced
- 2 cloves garlic, minced
- 2 tablespoons low-sodium soy sauce
- 1 tablespoon sesame oil
- 1 teaspoon ginger, grated (optional)
- 2 tablespoons olive oil
- Salt and pepper to taste

 4 servings |  15 minutes | 10 minutes

Directions:

1. Heat olive oil in a large skillet or wok over medium-high heat.
2. Add garlic and ginger, and sauté for 30 seconds.
3. Add broccoli, bell pepper, carrot, and zucchini. Stir-fry for 5 minutes.
4. Add shrimp and cook 3-4 minutes until they turn pink.
5. Stir in soy sauce and sesame oil, and cook for another minute.
6. Season with salt and pepper to taste.
7. Serve hot, garnished with sesame seeds if desired.

This Shrimp Stir-Fry with Vegetables is a colorful, nutritious, and delicious low-cholesterol dish, perfect for a healthy and satisfying meal. Combining lean protein from shrimp and various vegetables makes it an excellent option for a heart-healthy diet.

Nutritional Information: (per serving, approximate) Calories: 250, Protein: 25g, Carbohydrates: 10g, Fat: 12g, Fiber: 3g, Cholesterol: 180mg, Sodium: 350mg, Potassium: 400mg.

Seafood Paella with Brown Rice

Ingredients:

 **4** servings   **20** minutes   **40** minutes

- 1 cup brown rice
- 2 cups low-sodium chicken or vegetable broth
- 1/2 lb shrimp, peeled and deveined
- 1/2 lb scallops
- 1/2 lb mussels, cleaned and debearded
- 1 red bell pepper, sliced
- 1 onion, chopped
- 2 cloves garlic, minced
- 1 cup frozen peas
- 1 teaspoon paprika
- 1/2 teaspoon saffron threads
- 2 tablespoons olive oil
- Salt and pepper to taste
- Lemon wedges for serving

Directions:

1. Heat olive oil over medium heat in a large skillet or paella pan. Sauté onion, garlic, and bell pepper until softened.
2. Add brown rice, paprika, and saffron. Stir to combine and cook for 2 minutes.
3. Pour in the broth and bring to a simmer. Cover and cook for 30 minutes or until rice is almost tender.
4. Add shrimp, scallops, and mussels to the pan. Cover and cook for an additional 10 minutes, or until seafood is cooked and mussels have opened.
5. Stir in peas and cook for another 2 minutes.
6. Season with salt and pepper.
7. Serve hot, garnished with lemon wedges.

This Seafood Paella with Brown Rice is a hearty and flavorful low-cholesterol main dish, perfect for a nutritious and satisfying meal. It combines the goodness of whole grains with various seafood, making it an excellent choice for a heart-healthy diet.

Nutritional Information: (per serving, approximate) Calories: 350, Protein: 25g, Carbohydrates: 40g, Fat: 10g, Fiber: 4g, Cholesterol: 120mg, Sodium: 300mg, Potassium: 500mg.

Lemon-Garlic Tilapia with Asparagus

 **4** servings  **10** minutes   **20** minutes

Ingredients:

- 4 tilapia fillets (about 6 ounces each)
- 1 lb asparagus, trimmed
- 4 cloves garlic, minced
- Juice of 1 lemon
- Zest of 1 lemon
- 2 tablespoons olive oil
- Salt and pepper to taste
- Fresh parsley, chopped (for garnish)

Directions:

1. Preheat the oven to 400°F (200°C).
2. Arrange the tilapia fillets and asparagus in a single layer on a baking sheet.
3. Mix olive oil, garlic, lemon juice, and zest in a small bowl.
4. Brush the lemon-garlic mixture over the tilapia and asparagus. Season with salt and pepper.
5. Bake in the preheated oven for 15-20 minutes, until the tilapia is cooked and flakes easily with a fork, and asparagus is tender.
6. Garnish with fresh parsley and serve hot.

This Lemon-Garlic Tilapia with Asparagus is a light and healthy low-cholesterol main dish, combining the fresh flavors of lemon and garlic with the delicate taste of tilapia and the crunch of asparagus. It's perfect for a nutritious and easy-to-make meal.

Nutritional Information: (per serving, approximate) Calories: 220, Protein: 25g, Carbohydrates: 5g, Fat: 11g, Fiber: 2g, Cholesterol: 60mg, Sodium: 70mg, Potassium: 500mg.

Herb-Crusted Halibut with Roasted Vegetables

Ingredients:

- 4 halibut fillets (about 6 ounces each)
- 1 cup mixed fresh herbs (such as parsley, thyme, and basil), chopped
- 1 lemon, zest and juice
- 2 tablespoons olive oil
- 1 lb mixed vegetables (such as zucchini, bell peppers, and cherry tomatoes), chopped
- Salt and pepper to taste
- 2 cloves garlic, minced

 4 servings  15 minutes  25 minutes

Directions:

1. Preheat the oven to 400°F (200°C).
2. Combine chopped herbs, lemon zest, half lemon juice, and one tablespoon of olive oil in a bowl. Set aside.
3. Toss the chopped vegetables with olive oil, garlic, salt, and pepper. Spread them on a baking sheet and roast for 15 minutes.
4. Season halibut fillets with salt, pepper, and the remaining lemon juice.
5. Remove the vegetables from the oven and make space to place the halibut fillets on the same baking sheet.
6. Press the herb mixture onto the top of each halibut fillet.
7. Return the baking sheet to the oven and roast for 10 minutes until the fish is cooked and flakes easily.
8. Serve the herb-crusted halibut with the roasted vegetables.

This Herb-Crusted Halibut with Roasted Vegetables is a flavorful and nutritious low-cholesterol dish, perfect for a wholesome and satisfying meal. Combining fresh herbs and lemon enhances the natural flavors of the halibut and vegetables.

Nutritional Information: (per serving, approximate) Calories: 280, Protein: 30g, Carbohydrates: 10g, Fat: 13g, Fiber: 3g, Cholesterol: 55mg, Sodium: 150mg, Potassium: 800mg.

Pan-Seared Trout with Almond Butter

Ingredients:

- 4 trout fillets (about 6 ounces each)
- 1/4 cup slivered almonds
- 3 tablespoons unsalted butter
- Juice of 1 lemon
- Salt and pepper to taste
- 2 tablespoons olive oil
- Fresh parsley, chopped (for garnish)

This Pan-Seared Trout with Almond Butter is a simple yet elegant low-cholesterol dish that features the delicate flavor of trout enhanced with a rich and nutty almond butter sauce, making it a perfect choice for a heart-healthy meal.

 4 servings  10 minutes 15 minutes

Directions:

1. Season trout fillets with salt and pepper.
2. Heat olive oil in a large skillet over medium-high heat.
3. Add trout fillets, skin-side down, and cook for about 4-5 minutes until the skin is crispy.
4. Carefully flip the fillets and cook for 3-4 minutes until the fish is cooked.
5. Remove the trout from the skillet and keep warm.
6. In the same skillet, melt butter over medium heat. Add slivered almonds and cook until almonds are golden and the butter is slightly browned.
7. Remove from heat and stir in lemon juice.
8. Pour the almond butter sauce over the trout fillets.
9. Garnish with fresh parsley and serve immediately.

Nutritional Information: (per serving, approximate) Calories: 330, Protein: 28g, Carbohydrates: 2g, Fat: 24g, Fiber: 1g, Cholesterol: 85mg, Sodium: 100mg, Potassium: 500mg.

Fish Tacos with Cabbage Slaw

Ingredients:

- 1 lb white fish fillets (like cod or tilapia)
- 8 small corn tortillas
- 2 cups shredded cabbage
- 1 carrot, julienned
- 1/4 cup fresh cilantro, chopped (optional)
- Juice of 1 lime
- 1 tablespoon olive oil
- 1 teaspoon chili powder
- 1/2 teaspoon cumin (optional)
- Salt and pepper to taste
- For the Sauce:
- 1/2 cup low-fat Greek yogurt
- 1 tablespoon lime juice
- 1 teaspoon honey
- Salt to taste

 **4 servings** | **20 minutes** | **10 minutes**

Directions:

1. Mix Greek yogurt, lime juice, honey, and a pinch of salt in a small bowl to make the sauce. Set aside.
2. Combine shredded cabbage, carrot, cilantro, and lime juice in another bowl. Season with salt and pepper. Set the slaw aside.
3. Season fish fillets with chili powder, cumin, salt, and pepper.
4. Heat olive oil in a skillet over medium heat. Cook the fish on each side for 4-5 minutes until cooked through and easily flaked.
5. Warm the corn tortillas in a dry skillet or microwave.
6. To assemble tacos, place a portion of the fish on each tortilla, top with cabbage slaw, and drizzle with the yogurt sauce.
7. Serve immediately.

These Fish Tacos with Cabbage Slaw offer a perfect balance of flavors and textures, featuring flaky fish, crunchy slaw, and a creamy yogurt sauce, all wrapped in a soft tortilla. This dish is a delicious and heart-healthy option for a low-cholesterol diet.

Nutritional Information: (per serving, approximate) Calories: 280, Protein: 25g, Carbohydrates: 30g, Fat: 8g, Fiber: 5g, Cholesterol: 50mg, Sodium: 150mg, Potassium: 600mg.

Baked Haddock with Creamy Dill Sauce

 **4 servings** |  **10 minutes** | **15 minutes**

Ingredients:

- 4 haddock fillets (about 6 ounces each), (haddock can be substituted with cod or tilapia)
- 1/2 cup low-fat Greek yogurt
- 1 tablespoon fresh dill, chopped
- 1 tablespoon lemon juice
- 1 teaspoon Dijon mustard
- 1 clove garlic, minced
- Salt and pepper to taste
- Olive oil for greasing
- Lemon slices for garnish

Directions:

1. Preheat the oven to 400°F (200°C). Lightly grease a baking dish with olive oil.
2. Season the haddock fillets with salt and pepper and place them in the prepared baking dish.
3. Bake in the preheated oven for about 15 minutes or until the fish flakes easily with a fork.
4. Prepare the creamy dill sauce. In a small bowl, combine Greek yogurt, chopped dill, lemon juice, Dijon mustard, minced garlic, and a pinch of salt. Mix well until smooth.
5. Once the fish is done, remove it from the oven.
6. Serve the baked haddock with a generous dollop of the creamy dill sauce on top.
7. Garnish with lemon slices.

This Baked Haddock with Creamy Dill Sauce is a delightful low-cholesterol dish featuring tender haddock complemented by a tangy and herbaceous sauce. It's a simple yet elegant meal for weeknights and special occasions.

Nutritional Information: (per serving, approximate) Calories: 180, Protein: 28g, Carbohydrates: 3g, Fat: 6g, Fiber: 0g, Cholesterol: 80mg, Sodium: 150mg, Potassium: 600mg.

Grilled Salmon with Lemon and Herbs

Ingredients:

 4 servings  15 minutes  10 minutes

- 4 salmon fillets (about 6 ounces each)
- 2 lemons, one sliced and one juiced
- 2 tablespoons olive oil
- 1 tablespoon fresh dill, chopped
- 1 tablespoon fresh parsley, chopped
- 2 cloves garlic, minced
- Salt and pepper to taste

This Grilled Salmon with Lemon and Herbs is a healthy and delicious low-cholesterol dish, perfect for a nutritious and flavorful meal. The combination of fresh herbs and lemon enhances the natural taste of the salmon, making it a delightful option for any occasion.

Directions:

1. Mix olive oil, lemon juice, dill, parsley, garlic, salt, and pepper in a small bowl.
2. Place the salmon fillets in a dish and pour the herb mixture. Ensure each fillet is well-coated. Marinate for 10 minutes.
3. Preheat the grill to medium-high heat.
4. Grill the salmon fillets skin-side down for about 5 minutes.
5. Carefully flip the fillets and place lemon slices on top. Grill for 5 minutes until the salmon is cooked and flakes easily with a fork.
6. Remove from the grill and let rest for a few minutes.
7. Serve the grilled salmon with additional lemon slices and a sprinkle of fresh herbs.

Nutritional Information: (per serving, approximate) Calories: 280, Protein: 25g, Carbohydrates: 3g, Fat: 19g, Fiber: 1g, Cholesterol: 60mg, Sodium: 75mg, Potassium: 600mg.

Orange-Glazed Salmon with Asparagus

Ingredients:

 4 servings 15 minutes 20 minutes

- 4 salmon fillets (about 6 ounces each)
- 1 lb asparagus, trimmed
- 1 orange, zest and juice
- 2 tablespoons honey
- 1 tablespoon soy sauce (low sodium)
- 1 clove garlic, minced
- 2 tablespoons olive oil
- Salt and pepper to taste

This Orange-Glazed Salmon with Asparagus is a delightful low-cholesterol dish featuring a sweet and tangy glaze that complements the rich flavor of salmon. Paired with fresh asparagus, it makes for a nutritious and delicious meal.

Directions:

1. Preheat the oven to 400°F (200°C).
2. Add orange juice, honey, soy sauce, and garlic in a small bowl to make the glaze.
3. Place salmon fillets on a baking sheet lined with parchment paper. Brush the fillets with half of the orange glaze.
4. Toss asparagus with olive oil, orange zest, salt, and pepper. Arrange around the salmon on the baking sheet.
5. Bake in the preheated oven for 15-20 minutes or until the salmon is cooked and flakes easily with a fork.
6. Halfway through cooking, brush the remaining glaze over the salmon.
7. Serve the salmon and asparagus hot, drizzled with any remaining glaze.

Nutritional Information: (per serving, approximate) Calories: 310, Protein: 25g, Carbohydrates: 15g, Fat: 16g, Fiber: 3g, Cholesterol: 60mg, Sodium: 180mg, Potassium: 700mg.

Grilled Mahi-Mahi (dorado) with Mango Salsa

Ingredients:

 4 servings 20 minutes 10 minutes

- 4 Mahi-Mahi fillets (about 6 ounces each), (can be substituted with tuna or salmon)
- 2 tablespoons olive oil
- Salt and pepper to taste
- For the Mango Salsa:
- 1 ripe mango, diced
- 1/2 red bell pepper, diced
- 1/4 red onion, finely chopped
- 1 jalapeño, seeded and minced (optional)
- Juice of 1 lime
- 1 tablespoon cilantro, chopped
- Salt to taste

Directions:

1. Preheat the grill to medium-high heat.
2. Brush Mahi-Mahi fillets with olive oil and season with salt and pepper.
3. Grill the fillets on each side for 4-5 minutes or until the fish flakes easily with a fork.
4. While the fish is grilling, prepare the mango salsa. Combine diced mango, red bell pepper, red onion, jalapeno (if using), lime juice, and cilantro in a bowl. Season with salt and mix well.
5. Once the fish is cooked, remove it from the grill.
6. Serve the grilled Mahi-Mahi topped with a generous amount of mango salsa.
7. Garnish with additional cilantro if desired.

This Grilled Mahi-Mahi with Mango Salsa is a vibrant and flavorful low-cholesterol dish, perfect for a light and healthy meal. The tropical flavors of the mango salsa complement the mild taste of Mahi-Mahi, creating a delicious and nutritious combination.

Nutritional Information: (per serving, approximate) Calories: 240, Protein: 25g, Carbohydrates: 15g, Fat: 9g, Fiber: 2g, Cholesterol: 100mg, Sodium: 125mg, Potassium: 600mg.

Honey Garlic Baked Scallops

Ingredients:

 4 servings  10 minutes 15 minutes

- 1 lb sea scallops, rinsed and patted dry
- 3 tablespoons honey
- 2 cloves garlic, minced
- 1 tablespoon soy sauce (low sodium)
- 1 tablespoon lemon juice
- 2 tablespoons olive oil
- Salt and pepper to taste
- Fresh parsley, chopped (for garnish)

This Honey Garlic Baked Scallops dish is a simple yet elegant low-cholesterol recipe featuring scallops with a sweet and savory glaze. It's a perfect choice for a healthy and delicious meal that is easy to prepare and flavorful.

Directions:

1. Preheat the oven to 400°F (200°C).
2. Whisk together honey, minced garlic, soy sauce, and lemon juice in a small bowl.
3. Place the scallops in a baking dish. Drizzle them with olive oil and season with salt and pepper.
4. Spoon the honey garlic mixture over the scallops, making sure each one is well coated.
5. Bake in the oven for 12-15 minutes or until the scallops are cooked and have a slightly golden crust.
6. Remove from the oven and let rest for a few minutes.
7. Garnish with fresh parsley and serve immediately.

Nutritional Information: (per serving, approximate) Calories: 220, Protein: 20g, Carbohydrates: 18g, Fat: 8g, Fiber: 0g, Cholesterol: 35mg, Sodium: 320mg, Potassium: 350mg.

Crab Cakes with Remoulade Sauce

Ingredients:
For the Crab Cakes:

- 1 lb crabmeat, picked over for shells
- 1/4 cup whole wheat breadcrumbs
- 1/4 cup low-fat mayonnaise
- 1 egg, beaten
- 1 tablespoon Dijon mustard
- 1 tablespoon parsley, chopped
- 1 teaspoon Old Bay seasoning
- 1/4 teaspoon paprika
- Salt and pepper to taste
- 2 tablespoons olive oil for frying

 **4** servings **20** minutes **10** minutes

Directions:

1. Mix crabmeat, breadcrumbs, mayonnaise, beaten egg, Dijon mustard, parsley, Old Bay seasoning, paprika, salt, and pepper in a bowl.
2. Form the mixture into eight patties.
3. Heat olive oil in a skillet over medium heat.
4. Fry the crab cakes on each side for 4-5 minutes or until golden and cooked through.
5. In another bowl, mix all ingredients for the remoulade sauce.
6. Serve the hot crab cakes with a dollop of remoulade sauce on top.
7. Garnish with additional parsley if desired.

Ingredients:
For the Remoulade Sauce:

- 1/2 cup low-fat Greek yogurt
- 1 tablespoon Dijon mustard
- 1 tablespoon capers, chopped
- 1 tablespoon parsley, chopped
- 1 teaspoon lemon juice
- 1/2 teaspoon paprika
- Salt and pepper to taste

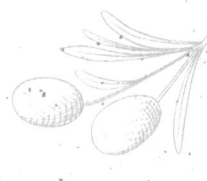

These Crab Cakes with Remoulade Sauce are a delightful low-cholesterol option, offering a perfect balance of savory crab meat and a tangy, creamy sauce. This dish is excellent for a light yet satisfying meal.

Nutritional Information: (per serving, approximate) Calories: 280, Protein: 25g, Carbohydrates: 10g, Fat: 15g, Fiber: 1g, Cholesterol: 95mg, Sodium: 450mg, Potassium: 350mg.

Pan-Seared Cod
with Parsley Cauliflower Rice

 4 servings    15 minutes   20 minutes

Ingredients:

- 4 cod fillets (6 ounces each)
- 1 head of cauliflower, grated or processed into rice-sized pieces
- 2 tablespoons olive oil
- 1/4 cup fresh parsley, chopped
- 2 cloves garlic, minced
- Juice of 1 lemon
- Salt and pepper to taste

Directions:

1. Season the cod fillets with salt and pepper on both sides.
2. Heat one tablespoon of olive oil in a large skillet over medium-high heat. Add the cod fillets and cook for about 4 minutes on each side or until cooked through and golden brown. Remove from the skillet and set aside.
3. Add the remaining tablespoon of olive oil and minced garlic in the same skillet. Roast for about 1 minute or until fragrant.
4. Add the grated cauliflower to the skillet, stirring to combine with the garlic. Cook for about 5-7 minutes or until the cauliflower is tender.
5. Remove the skillet from heat and stir in the chopped parsley and lemon juice. Season with salt and pepper to taste.
6. Serve the pan-seared cod over a bed of parsley cauliflower rice, garnishing with lemon slices if desired.

This Pan-Seared Cod with Parsley Cauliflower Rice recipe offers a healthy, low-cholesterol dinner option that is both flavorful and satisfying. The lean protein from the cod pairs beautifully with the light and fresh cauliflower rice, making it a perfect meal for maintaining a heart-healthy diet.

Nutritional Information (per serving, approximate): Calories: 250, Protein: 28g, Carbohydrates: 8g, Fat: 12g, Fiber: 3g, Cholesterol: 60mg, Sodium: 200mg, Potassium: 650mg.

Chicken Cacciatore with Whole Wheat Pasta

Ingredients:

 4 servings  15 minutes  30 minutes

- 4 boneless, skinless chicken breasts
- 1 cup whole wheat pasta
- 2 cups low-sodium tomato sauce
- 1 bell pepper, sliced
- 1 onion, chopped
- 2 cloves garlic, minced
- 1/2 cup mushrooms, sliced
- 1/2 cup low-sodium chicken broth
- 2 tablespoons olive oil
- 1 teaspoon dried oregano
- 1 teaspoon dried basil
- Salt and pepper to taste
- Fresh parsley, chopped (for garnish)
- Grated Parmesan cheese (optional for serving)

Directions:

1. Season the chicken breasts with salt, pepper, oregano, and basil.
2. Heat olive oil in a large skillet over medium heat. Add the chicken and cook until browned on both sides. Remove from the skillet and set aside.
3. Add onion, bell pepper, garlic, and mushrooms in the same skillet. Cook until the vegetables are softened.
4. Add the tomato sauce and chicken broth to the skillet and stir to combine.
5. Return the chicken to the skillet, cover, and simmer for 20 minutes.
6. While the chicken is cooking, cook the whole wheat pasta according to package instructions until al dente.
7. If desired, serve the chicken cacciatore over the cooked pasta, garnished with fresh parsley and grated Parmesan cheese.

This Chicken Cacciatore with Whole Wheat Pasta is a hearty, flavorful, low-cholesterol dish, combining tender chicken, nutritious vegetables, and wholesome whole wheat pasta in a rich tomato sauce. It's a balanced and satisfying meal that is perfect for any day of the week.

Nutritional Information: (per serving, approximate) Calories: 350, Protein: 30g, Carbohydrates: 35g, Fat: 10g, Fiber: 6g, Cholesterol: 65mg, Sodium: 300mg, Potassium: 600mg.

Chicken Fajitas
with Bell Peppers and Onions

 4 servings   20 minutes   15 minutes

Ingredients:

- 1 lb boneless, skinless chicken breasts cut into thin strips
- 2 bell peppers (any color), sliced
- 1 large onion, sliced
- 2 cloves garlic, minced
- 2 tablespoons olive oil
- Juice of 1 lime
- 1 teaspoon chili powder (optional)
- 1/2 teaspoon cumin (optional)
- 1/2 teaspoon paprika
- Salt and pepper to taste
- 8 whole wheat tortillas
- Fresh cilantro, chopped (for garnish)
- For the Greek Yogurt Sauce:
- 1/2 cup low-fat Greek yogurt
- 1 tablespoon lime juice
- 1/2 teaspoon garlic powder
- Salt and pepper to taste

Directions:

1. Mix Greek yogurt, lime juice, garlic powder, salt, and pepper in a small bowl to make the sauce. Set aside.
2. Combine lime juice, chili powder, cumin, paprika, salt, and pepper in another bowl. Add the chicken strips and toss to coat. Set aside to marinate for 10 minutes.
3. Heat 1 tablespoon olive oil in a large skillet over medium-high heat. Add the bell peppers and onion, cooking until they are soft and slightly charred. Remove from the skillet and set aside.
4. Add the remaining olive oil and marinated chicken strips in the same skillet. Cook until the chicken is fully cooked and slightly browned.
5. Return the bell peppers and onion to the skillet with the chicken. Stir to combine and heat through.
6. Warm the whole wheat tortillas in a dry skillet or microwave.
7. Spoon the chicken and vegetable mixture into the tortillas to assemble the fajitas.
8. Drizzle with Greek yogurt sauce and garnish with chopped cilantro.

Chicken Fajitas with Bell Peppers and Onions is a colorful and flavorful dish that brings together tender chicken strips, crisp bell peppers, and sweet onions, all seasoned with a blend of spices. This low-cholesterol recipe is easy to prepare and nutritious, making it a perfect addition to a heart-healthy diet.

Nutritional Information: (per serving, approximate) Calories: 360, Protein: 30g, Carbohydrates: 38g, Fat: 13g, Fiber: 6g, Cholesterol: 65mg, Sodium: 330mg, Potassium: 520mg.

Greek Yogurt Sauce with Avocado Cream
(Chicken Fajitas with Bell Peppers and Onions)

 4 servings    5 minutes    0 minutes

Ingredients:

- 1 ripe avocado, peeled and pitted
- 1/4 cup plain Greek yogurt (or non-dairy yogurt for a vegan option)
- 1 tablespoon freshly squeezed lime juice
- 1 clove garlic, minced
- 2 tablespoons chopped fresh cilantro
- Salt and black pepper to taste

Directions:

1. In a bowl, mash the ripe avocado with a fork until smooth.
2. Add the plain Greek yogurt, freshly squeezed lime juice, minced garlic, chopped fresh cilantro, salt, and black pepper to the mashed avocado.
3. Mix all the ingredients until well combined and creamy.
4. Taste the avocado cream and adjust the seasoning if necessary, adding more salt, pepper, or lime juice to suit your taste preferences.
5. Transfer the avocado cream to a serving bowl or container.

Nutritional Information: (per serving, approximate) Calories: 70, Protein: 2g, Carbohydrates: 5g, Fat: 5g, Fiber: 3g, Cholesterol: 0mg, Sodium: 10mg, Potassium: 240mg.

Nutritional Information: (per serving, approximate) Calories: 280, Protein: 7g, Carbohydrates: 40g, Fat: 12g, Fiber: 4g, Cholesterol: 0mg, Sodium: 10mg, Potassium: 250mg.

Rosemary Garlic Roasted Turkey Breast

 4 servings   15 minutes   45 minutes

Ingredients:

- 2 lbs turkey breast, boneless and skinless
- 4 cloves garlic, minced
- 2 tablespoons fresh rosemary, chopped
- 2 tablespoons olive oil
- Juice of 1 lemon
- Salt and pepper to taste

Directions:

1. Preheat the oven to 375°F (190°C).
2. In a small bowl, combine minced garlic, chopped rosemary, olive oil, lemon juice, salt, and pepper to create a marinade.
3. Rub the marinade thoroughly over the turkey breast, ensuring it coats evenly.
4. Place the marinated turkey breast in a roasting pan.
5. Roast in the oven for about 45 minutes or until the turkey is fully cooked. The internal temperature should reach 165°F (74°C) when checked with a meat thermometer.
6. Remove the turkey breast from the oven and let it rest for a few minutes before slicing.
7. Serve the sliced turkey breast with your choice of side dishes.

Rosemary Garlic Roasted Turkey Breast is an aromatic and succulent dish that combines the rich flavors of fresh rosemary and garlic with lean turkey breast. This low-cholesterol recipe offers a delicious way to enjoy a classic roast, making it an ideal choice for a healthy, flavorful meal that's sure to impress.

Nutritional Information: (per serving, approximate) Calories: 230, Protein: 35g, Carbohydrates: 2g, Fat: 9g, Fiber: 0g, Cholesterol: 85mg, Sodium: 110mg, Potassium: 300mg.

Beef and Mushroom Stroganoff

 **4** servings   **20** minutes   **30** minutes

Ingredients:

- 1 lb lean beef sirloin, thinly sliced
- 2 cups mushrooms, sliced
- 1 onion, chopped
- 2 cloves garlic, minced
- 1 cup low-sodium beef broth
- 1/2 cup low-fat sour cream
- 2 tablespoons whole wheat flour
- 1 tablespoon olive oil
- 1 teaspoon paprika
- Salt and pepper to taste
- 2 tablespoons fresh parsley, chopped
- 8 oz whole wheat egg noodles, cooked

Directions:

1. Heat olive oil in a large skillet over medium heat. Add the beef and cook until browned. Remove from the skillet and set aside.
2. In the same skillet, add onions and garlic. Cook until softened.
3. Add mushrooms to the skillet and cook until they release their moisture and begin to brown.
4. Sprinkle whole wheat flour over the vegetables and stir to coat. Cook for 1 minute.
5. Gradually add beef broth, stirring constantly to avoid lumps. Bring to a simmer.
6. Return the beef to the skillet and add paprika, salt, and pepper. Simmer for 10 minutes.
7. Reduce heat to low and stir in low-fat sour cream. Heat through without boiling.
8. Serve the stroganoff over cooked whole wheat egg noodles, garnished with fresh parsley.

This Beef and Mushroom Stroganoff recipe is a low-cholesterol version of the classic dish. It uses lean beef sirloin, low-fat sour cream to reduce fat content and whole wheat flour and egg noodles for added fiber. The dish maintains its creamy and savory flavor while being more heart-healthy.

Nutritional Information: (per serving, approximate) Calories: 390, Protein: 32g, Carbohydrates: 40g, Fat: 12g, Fiber: 5g, Cholesterol: 85mg, Sodium: 180mg, Potassium: 700mg.

Chicken Piccata with Capers

 4 servings  10 minutes  20 minutes

Ingredients:

- 4 boneless, skinless chicken breasts, thinly sliced or pounded
- 1/4 cup whole wheat flour
- 2 tablespoons olive oil
- Juice of 1 lemon
- 1/2 cup low-sodium chicken broth
- 2 tablespoons capers, drained
- 2 cloves garlic, minced
- 1 tablespoon fresh parsley, chopped
- Salt and pepper to taste
- Lemon slices for garnish

Directions:

1. Season the chicken breasts with salt and pepper. Dredge them lightly in whole wheat flour, shaking off the excess.
2. Heat olive oil in a large skillet over medium-high heat. Add the chicken breasts and cook until golden brown on both sides and cooked through, about 3-4 minutes per side. Remove chicken from the skillet and set aside.
3. In the same skillet, add garlic and cook for about 1 minute until fragrant.
4. Add lemon juice and chicken broth to the skillet, scraping up any browned bits from the bottom of the pan.
5. tir in capers and return the chicken to the skillet. Cook for 2-3 minutes, allowing the sauce to thicken slightly and the flavors to blend.
6. Remove from heat and sprinkle with fresh parsley.
7. Serve the chicken piccata garnished with lemon slices.

This low-cholesterol Chicken Piccata with Capers is a light and flavorful dish perfect for a healthy diet. The combination of lemon, capers, and garlic provides a zesty and refreshing taste, while using whole-wheat flour for dredging adds a nutritious touch. This meal is ideal for those who enjoy a classic Italian dish with a healthier twist.

Nutritional Information: (per serving, approximate) Calories: 230, Protein: 26g, Carbohydrates: 8g, Fat: 10g, Fiber: 1g, Cholesterol: 65mg, Sodium: 220mg, Potassium: 300mg.

Grilled Lamb Chops with Mint Pesto

 **4** servings   **20** minutes   **10** minutes

Ingredients:

- 8 lamb chops (lean, trimmed of excess fat)
- Salt and pepper to taste
- For the Mint Pesto:
- 1 cup fresh mint leaves
- 1/4 cup parsley leaves
- 2 cloves garlic
- 1/4 cup walnuts
- Juice of 1 lemon
- 1/4 cup olive oil
- Salt and pepper to taste

Directions:

1. In a food processor, combine mint leaves, parsley, garlic, walnuts, and lemon juice for the mint pesto. Process until finely chopped.
2. With the food processor running, slowly add olive oil until the mixture becomes a smooth paste. Season with salt and pepper to taste. Set aside.
3. Preheat the grill to medium-high heat.
4. Season lamb chops with salt and pepper.
5. Grill the lamb chops for 4-5 minutes on each side or until they reach the desired level of doneness.
6. Remove lamb chops from the grill and let them rest for a few minutes.
7. Serve the grilled lamb chops with a dollop of mint pesto on top

This low-cholesterol recipe for Grilled Lamb Chops with Mint Pesto is flavorful and heart-healthy. The lean lamb chops provide an excellent source of protein, while the mint pesto adds a fresh and herby flavor without adding cholesterol. The use of olive oil, rich in monounsaturated fats, and walnuts, high in omega-3 fatty acids, makes the pesto a healthy addition to the dish.

Nutritional Information: (per serving, approximate) Calories: 380, Protein: 24g, Carbohydrates: 2g, Fat: 30g, Fiber: 1g, Cholesterol: 70mg, Sodium: 200mg, Potassium: 350mg.

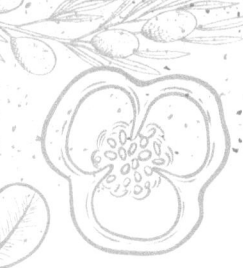

Pork Chops with Apple Cider Vinegar Sauce

 4 servings | 15 minutes | 25 minutes

Ingredients:

- 4 boneless pork chops (lean, trimmed of excess fat)
- Salt and pepper to taste
- 1 tablespoon olive oil
- 2 apples, cored and sliced
- 1 onion, thinly sliced
- 2 cloves garlic, minced
- 1/2 cup low-sodium chicken broth
- 1/4 cup apple cider vinegar
- 1 tablespoon Dijon mustard
- 1 teaspoon fresh thyme leaves (optional)
- 1 tablespoon honey (optional)

Directions:

1. Season pork chops with salt and pepper.
2. Heat olive oil in a large skillet over medium-high heat. Add pork chops and cook until golden brown on both sides and cook through for about 5-6 minutes per side. Remove pork chops from the skillet and set aside.
3. In the same skillet, add sliced apples and onions. Cook until the onion is translucent and the apples are slightly softened about 5 minutes.
4. Add garlic to the skillet and cook for an additional minute.
5. Pour in chicken broth and apple cider vinegar. Stir in Dijon mustard, thyme, and honey (if using). Bring to a simmer.
6. Return pork chops to the skillet. Cook for 2-3 minutes, thickening the sauce and coating the pork chops.
7. Serve the pork chops topped with apple cider vinegar sauce.

This Pork Chops with Apple Cider Vinegar Sauce recipe offers a low-cholesterol option that does not compromise flavor. Lean pork chops and heart-healthy olive oil suit those who monitor their cholesterol levels. Combining tart apple cider vinegar and sweet apples creates a deliciously balanced sauce that complements the pork perfectly.

Nutritional Information: (per serving, approximate) Calories: 310, Protein: 25g, Carbohydrates: 15g, Fat: 16g, Fiber: 2g, Cholesterol: 65mg, Sodium: 200mg, Potassium: 500mg.

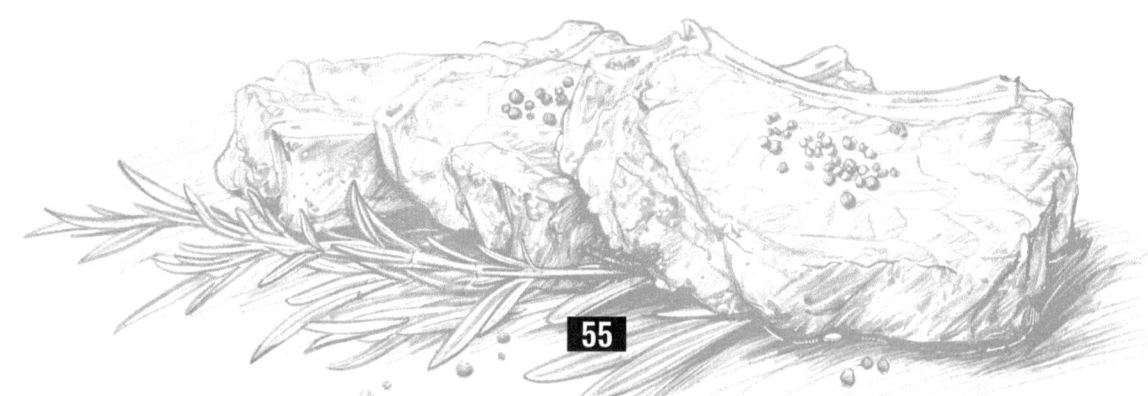

Lean Beef and Broccoli Stir-Fry

 4 servings | 15 minutes | 15 minutes

Ingredients:

- 1 lb lean beef sirloin, thinly sliced
- 4 cups broccoli florets
- 1 bell pepper, sliced
- 1 onion, thinly sliced
- 2 cloves garlic, minced
- 2 tablespoons olive oil
- For the Sauce:
- 1/3 cup low-sodium soy sauce
- 1/4 cup water
- 2 tablespoons cornstarch
- 1 tablespoon honey
- 1 teaspoon ground ginger
- 1 teaspoon sesame oil

Directions:

1. Season pork chops with salt and pepper.
2. Heat olive oil in a large skillet over medium-high heat. Add pork chops and cook until golden brown on both sides and cook through for about 5-6 minutes per side. Remove pork chops from the skillet and set aside.
3. In the same skillet, add sliced apples and onions. Cook until the onion is translucent and the apples are slightly softened about 5 minutes.
4. Add garlic to the skillet and cook for an additional minute.
5. Pour in chicken broth and apple cider vinegar. Stir in Dijon mustard, thyme, and honey (if using). Bring to a simmer.
6. Return pork chops to the skillet. Cook for 2-3 minutes, thickening the sauce and coating the pork chops.
7. Serve the pork chops topped with apple cider vinegar sauce.

This Lean Beef and Broccoli Stir-Fry is a healthy and flavorful dish perfect for a low-cholesterol diet. Using lean beef sirloin and plenty of fresh vegetables, it's packed with protein and nutrients. The sauce adds a rich and savory dimension without the excess sodium often found in traditional stir-fry dishes.

Nutritional Information: (per serving, approximate) Calories: 280, Protein: 26g, Carbohydrates: 16g, Fat: 12g, Fiber: 3g, Cholesterol: 55mg, Sodium: 420mg, Potassium: 650mg.

Balsamic Glazed Pork Tenderloin

Ingredients:

 4 servings   10 minutes   25 minutes

- 1 pork tenderloin (about 1 lb), trimmed of fat
- Salt and pepper to taste
- 2 tablespoons olive oil
- For the Glaze:
- 1/3 cup balsamic vinegar
- 2 tablespoons honey
- 1 tablespoon Dijon mustard
- 2 cloves garlic, minced
- 1 teaspoon rosemary, finely chopped

Directions:

1. Preheat oven to 375°F (190°C).
2. Season the pork tenderloin with salt and pepper.
3. Heat olive oil in an oven-proof skillet over medium-high heat. Add the pork tenderloin and sear on all sides until golden brown, about 2-3 minutes per side.
4. In a small bowl, whisk together balsamic vinegar, honey, Dijon mustard, minced garlic, and rosemary to create the glaze.
5. Brush the glaze over the seared pork tenderloin.
6. Place the skillet in the preheated oven and roast the pork for 15-20 minutes until it reaches an internal temperature of 145°F (63°C).
7. Remove from the oven and let the pork rest for 5 minutes before slicing.
8. Serve the sliced pork tenderloin with additional balsamic glaze drizzled on top.

This low-cholesterol Balsamic Glazed Pork Tenderloin recipe is delicious and elegant. The lean pork tenderloin creates a satisfying, heart-healthy meal paired with the rich and flavorful balsamic glaze. The dish is simple to prepare yet impressive enough for a special occasion!

Nutritional Information: (per serving, approximate) Calories: 240, Protein: 24g, Carbohydrates: 10g, Fat: 11g, Fiber: 0g, Cholesterol: 70mg, Sodium: 200mg, Potassium: 450mg.

Chicken and Vegetable Kebabs

 4 servings | 20 minutes | 10 minutes

Ingredients:

- 2 boneless, skinless chicken breasts cut into 1-inch cubes
- 1 zucchini, sliced into 1/2-inch rounds
- 1 red bell pepper, cut into 1-inch pieces
- 1 yellow bell pepper, cut into 1-inch pieces
- 1 red onion, cut into chunks
- 8 wooden or metal skewers
- For the Marinade:
- 1/4 cup olive oil
- 2 tablespoons lemon juice
- 2 cloves garlic, minced
- 1 teaspoon dried oregano
- 1 teaspoon dried thyme
- Salt and pepper to taste

Directions:

1. Add olive oil, lemon juice, minced garlic, oregano, thyme, salt, and pepper to make the marinade in a bowl.
2. Place the chicken cubes in the marinade and stir to coat evenly. Refrigerate for at least 30 minutes or up to 2 hours.
3. If using wooden skewers, soak them in water for 30 minutes to prevent burning.
4. Preheat the grill to medium-high heat.
5. Thread the marinated chicken, zucchini, bell peppers, and red onion onto the skewers, alternating the ingredients.
6. Grill the kebabs on each side for 4-5 minutes or until the chicken is fully cooked and the vegetables are tender.
7. Serve the chicken and vegetable kebabs hot.

This low-cholesterol Chicken and Vegetable Kebabs recipe is a healthy and delicious option for grilling. The chicken and various colorful vegetables make it a nutritious and visually appealing meal. The marinade adds excellent flavor to the chicken and vegetables without adding excessive calories or cholesterol. This dish is perfect for a summer barbecue or a family dinner.

Nutritional Information: (per serving, approximate) Calories: 220, Protein: 24g, Carbohydrates: 9g, Fat: 10g, Fiber: 2g, Cholesterol: 55mg, Sodium: 100mg, Potassium: 500mg.

Baked Turkey Meatballs with Tomato Basil Sauce

 4 servings 20 minutes 30 minutes

Ingredients:

For the Meatballs:
- 1 lb ground turkey (lean)
- 1/2 cup whole wheat breadcrumbs
- 1/4 cup grated Parmesan cheese
- 1 egg, beaten
- 2 cloves garlic, minced
- 2 tablespoons fresh parsley, chopped
- Salt and pepper to taste
- For the Tomato Basil Sauce:
- 1 can (28 oz) crushed tomatoes
- 1 onion, finely chopped
- 2 cloves garlic, minced
- 2 tablespoons olive oil
- 1/4 cup fresh basil, chopped
- Salt and pepper to taste

Directions:

1. Preheat the oven to 400°F (200°C). Line a baking sheet with parchment paper.
2. Combine ground turkey, breadcrumbs, Parmesan cheese, beaten egg, minced garlic, parsley, salt, and pepper in a large bowl. Mix well.
3. Place the mixture into 1-inch meatballs on the prepared baking sheet.
4. Bake the meatballs in the oven for 20 minutes or until cooked.
5. While the meatballs are baking, prepare the sauce. In a large saucepan, heat olive oil over medium heat. Add chopped onion and minced garlic, and sauté until softened.
6. Add crushed tomatoes to the saucepan. Bring to a simmer and cook for 10 minutes.
7. Add chopped basil, salt, and pepper to the tomato sauce.
8. Once the meatballs are cooked, add them to the tomato basil sauce and gently stir to coat.
9. Serve the meatballs and sauce hot, garnished with additional fresh basil or Parmesan cheese if desired.

These Baked Turkey Meatballs with Tomato Basil Sauce are a heart-healthy option for a low-cholesterol diet. Using lean ground turkey and whole wheat breadcrumbs, the meatballs are flavorful yet low in saturated fat and cholesterol. The homemade tomato basil sauce adds a fresh and vibrant touch to the dish, making it a nutritious and comforting meal.

Nutritional Information: (per serving, approximate) Calories: 320, Protein: 28g, Carbohydrates: 18g, Fat: 15g, Fiber: 3g, Cholesterol: 110mg, Sodium: 400mg, Potassium: 500mg.

Turkey and Vegetable Stir-Fry with Homemade Stir-Fry Sauce

 4 servings 15 minutes 15 minutes

Ingredients:

- 1 lb ground turkey (lean)
- 1 red bell pepper, sliced
- 1 green bell pepper, sliced
- 1 medium zucchini, sliced
- 1 medium carrot, julienned
- 1 onion, sliced
- 2 cloves garlic, minced
- 2 tablespoons olive oil
- For the Homemade Stir-Fry Sauce:
- 1/4 cup low-sodium soy sauce
- 1 tablespoon sesame oil
- 2 tablespoons rice vinegar
- 1 tablespoon honey
- 1 teaspoon ginger, grated
- 1 teaspoon cornstarch
- 1/4 cup water

Directions:

1. To make the stir-fry sauce, whisk together soy sauce, sesame oil, rice vinegar, honey, and grated ginger in a small bowl. Mix cornstarch with 1/4 cup of water in another small bowl until smooth. Combine the cornstarch mixture with the soy sauce mixture and set aside.
2. Heat 1 tablespoon of olive oil in a large skillet or wok over medium-high heat. Add ground turkey and cook until browned and cooked through, breaking it into crumbles, about 5-7 minutes. Remove the turkey from the skillet and set aside.
3. In the same skillet, heat the remaining olive oil. Add red and green bell peppers, zucchini, carrot, onion, and garlic. Stir-fry until the vegetables are tender-crisp, about 5 minutes.
4. Return the cooked turkey to the skillet with the vegetables.
5. Pour the homemade stir-fry sauce over the turkey and vegetables. Stir well to combine and cook for 2-3 minutes until the sauce is heated and thickens.
6. If desired, serve the stir-fry hot, garnished with sesame seeds or green onions.

This Turkey and Vegetable Stir-Fry recipe includes a homemade stir-fry sauce that adds a rich and flavorful dimension. The combination of lean ground turkey and fresh vegetables makes this meal delicious and suitable for a low-cholesterol diet. The homemade sauce ensures you can control the ingredients and avoid excess sodium and preservatives in store-bought versions.

Nutritional Information: (per serving, approximate) Calories: 270, Protein: 27g, Carbohydrates: 15g, Fat: 12g, Fiber: 3g, Cholesterol: 60mg, Sodium: 420mg, Potassium: 600mg.

Balsamic Glazed Chicken Drumsticks

 **4** servings | **10** minutes | **40** minutes

Ingredients:

- 8 chicken drumsticks, skin removed
- Salt and pepper to taste
- 1/4 cup balsamic vinegar
- 2 tablespoons honey
- 1 tablespoon Dijon mustard
- 2 cloves garlic, minced
- 1 teaspoon dried rosemary
- 1 teaspoon dried thyme (optional)
- Olive oil spray

Directions:

1. Preheat the oven to 375°F (190°C). Line a baking sheet with aluminum foil and place a wire rack on top. Spray the rack with olive oil spray.
2. Season the chicken drumsticks with salt and pepper and arrange them on the wire rack.
3. Combine balsamic vinegar, honey, Dijon mustard, minced garlic, rosemary, and thyme in a small saucepan over medium heat. Bring the mixture to a simmer, stirring occasionally, and cook until slightly thickened, about 5-7 minutes.
4. Brush the chicken drumsticks with the balsamic glaze, coating them evenly.
5. Bake the chicken in the preheated oven for 20 minutes. Remove from the oven, brush with more glaze, and return to the oven. Bake for an additional 20 minutes or until the chicken is fully cooked and the internal temperature reaches 165°F (74°C).
6. Serve the chicken drumsticks hot, garnished with additional fresh herbs if desired.

These low-cholesterol Balsamic Glazed Chicken Drumsticks are a delicious and healthy option for a main course. By removing the skin from the drumsticks, you significantly reduce the saturated fat and cholesterol content. The balsamic glaze provides a rich, tangy flavor that pairs perfectly with the tender chicken. This dish is easy to prepare and visually appealing, making it an excellent choice for family dinners and special occasions.

Nutritional Information: (per serving, approximate) Calories: 220, Protein: 28g, Carbohydrates: 10g, Fat: 8g, Fiber: 0g, Cholesterol: 100mg, Sodium: 200mg, Potassium: 300mg.

Turkey Chili with Beans and Vegetables

🍲 6 servings | 🕐 20 minutes | ⏱️ 40 minutes

Ingredients:

- 1 lb ground turkey breast (lean)
- 1 can (15 oz) kidney beans, drained and rinsed
- 1 can (15 oz) black beans, drained and rinsed
- 1 large onion, chopped
- 1 red bell pepper, chopped
- 1 green bell pepper, chopped
- 2 carrots, diced
- 2 cloves garlic, minced
- 1 can (28 oz) diced tomatoes with juice
- 2 tablespoons tomato paste
- 2 cups low-sodium chicken or vegetable broth
- 1 tablespoon chili powder
- 1 teaspoon cumin (optional)
- 1 teaspoon paprika
- 1/2 teaspoon dried oregano
- Salt and pepper to taste
- Olive oil for cooking

Directions:

1. Heat a large pot over medium heat and add a drizzle of olive oil.
2. Add the ground turkey to the pot and cook until browned, then break it up with a spoon for about 5-7 minutes.
3. Add the chopped onion, bell peppers, carrots, and garlic to the pot. Cook for an additional 5 minutes until the vegetables begin to soften.
4. Stir in the chili powder, cumin, paprika, and oregano. Cook for 1 minute to release the flavors.
5. Add the diced tomatoes, tomato paste, kidney beans, black beans, and chicken or vegetable broth to the pot. Season with salt and pepper.
6. Bring the chili to a simmer, reduce the heat to low, and cover. Let it cook for 30 minutes, stirring occasionally.
7. Taste and adjust seasoning if necessary. If desired, serve hot, garnished with fresh cilantro, shredded cheese, or a dollop of Greek yogurt.

This low-cholesterol Turkey Chili with Beans and Vegetables is hearty and nutritious, perfect for a cozy dinner. It's packed with lean protein from the ground turkey, fiber from the beans and vegetables, and rich in flavors from the blend of spices. This chili is an excellent option for those watching their cholesterol levels, as it uses lean turkey and includes plenty of vegetables for added health benefits.

Nutritional Information: (per serving, approximate) Calories: 280, Protein: 26g, Carbohydrates: 35g, Fat: 6g, Fiber: 10g, Cholesterol: 45mg, Sodium: 300mg, Potassium: 800mg.

Mediterranean Turkey Stuffed Peppers

 6 servings | 20 minutes | 30 minutes

Ingredients:

- 4 large bell peppers (any color), tops cut off and seeds removed
- 1 lb ground turkey breast (lean)
- 1 cup cooked quinoa
- 1 can (14.5 oz) diced tomatoes, drained
- 1 small onion, chopped
- 2 cloves garlic, minced
- 1/4 cup chopped fresh parsley
- 1/4 cup crumbled feta cheese
- 2 tablespoons olive oil
- 1 teaspoon dried oregano
- 1/2 teaspoon paprika
- Salt and pepper to taste

Directions:

1. Preheat the oven to 375°F (190°C).
2. In a skillet over medium heat, heat one tablespoon of olive oil. Add the chopped onion and garlic, and saute until softened for 3-4 minutes.
3. Add the ground turkey to the skillet. Cook until the turkey is browned and cooked, breaking it up with a spoon for 5-7 minutes.
4. Stir in the cooked quinoa, diced tomatoes, parsley, oregano, paprika, salt, and pepper. Cook for another 2-3 minutes, then remove from heat.
5. Drizzle the inside of the bell peppers with the remaining olive oil and season with a bit of salt and pepper.
6. Fill each pepper with the turkey and quinoa mixture. Place the stuffed peppers in a baking dish and cover with foil.
7. Bake in the oven for 25-30 minutes or until the peppers are tender.
8. Remove from the oven, sprinkle the tops with crumbled feta cheese, and serve.

These low-cholesterol Mediterranean Turkey Stuffed Peppers are healthy and flavorful, perfect for a nutritious meal. The lean ground turkey and quinoa provide a high-protein, low-fat stuffing, while the bell peppers add a good dose of vitamins and fiber. Adding feta cheese, herbs, and spices brings a delightful Mediterranean flair to the dish, making it both heart-healthy and delicious.

Nutritional Information: (per serving, approximate) Calories: 320, Protein: 28g, Carbohydrates: 24g, Fat: 12g, Fiber: 5g, Cholesterol: 60mg, Sodium: 300mg, Potassium: 700mg.

Low-Cholesterol Turkey Burger with Avocado and Spinach

 **4** servings **15** minutes **10** minutes

Ingredients:

- 1 lb ground turkey breast (lean)
- 1 ripe avocado, sliced
- 1 cup fresh spinach leaves
- 4 whole wheat hamburger buns
- 1/4 cup low-fat Greek yogurt
- 1 tablespoon Dijon mustard
- 1 clove garlic, minced
- 1/2 small red onion, finely chopped
- 1 teaspoon smoked paprika
- Salt and pepper to taste
- Olive oil for grilling

Directions:

1. Combine the ground turkey, minced garlic, chopped red onion, smoked paprika, salt, and pepper in a large bowl. Mix well.
2. Divide the turkey mixture into four equal portions and shape each into a burger patty.
3. Preheat a grill or grill pan over medium heat. Lightly brush the grill with olive oil.
4. Grill the turkey patties for about 5 minutes on each side or until fully cooked (internal temperature should reach 165°F or 74°C).
5. Mix the Greek yogurt and Dijon mustard in a small bowl while grilling the patties to create a healthy, creamy spread.
6. Toast the whole wheat hamburger buns lightly on the grill.
7. To assemble the burgers, spread the Greek yogurt mixture on the bottom half of each bun. Place a grilled turkey patty on top, followed by a few spinach leaves and avocado slices.
8. Cover with the top half of the bun and serve immediately.

This Low-Cholesterol Turkey Burger with Avocado and Spinach is a healthy alternative to traditional beef burgers. Using lean ground turkey and whole wheat buns significantly reduces the saturated fat and cholesterol content. The addition of avocado provides healthy fats, while spinach adds a boost of nutrients. The Greek yogurt and Dijon mustard spread is a delicious and low-fat alternative to mayonnaise, making this burger heart-healthy and flavorful.

Nutritional Information: (per serving, approximate) Calories: 350, Protein: 28g, Carbohydrates: 27g, Fat: 15g, Fiber: 6g, Cholesterol: 60mg, Sodium: 320mg, Potassium: 500mg.

Chicken Mini Meatballs

 **4** servings   **15** minutes   **20** minutes

Ingredients:

- 1 pound ground chicken breast
- 1/4 cup breadcrumbs (whole wheat, if available)
- 1/4 cup grated Parmesan cheese (reduced-fat, if available)
- 1 egg
- 2 cloves garlic, minced
- 2 tablespoons fresh parsley, chopped
- 1/2 teaspoon dried oregano
- Salt and black pepper to taste
- Cooking spray or olive oil for greasing

Directions:

1. Preheat the oven to 400°F (200°C). Lightly grease a baking sheet with cooking spray or olive oil.
2. Combine the ground chicken breast, breadcrumbs, grated Parmesan cheese, egg, minced garlic, chopped parsley, dried oregano, salt, and black pepper in a large mixing bowl. Mix well until all ingredients are evenly incorporated.
3. Take small portions of the mixture and roll them into mini meatballs, about 1 inch in diameter, and place them on the prepared baking sheet.
4. Once all the mini meatballs are formed, place the baking sheet in the preheated oven and bake for 15-20 minutes, or until the meatballs are cooked through and golden brown.
5. Remove the baking sheet from the oven and let the meatballs cool slightly before serving.

Serve the Low-Cholesterol Chicken Mini Meatballs as a delicious and protein-packed addition to your favorite dishes.

Nutritional Information: (per serving, approximate) Calories: 200, Protein: 25g, Carbohydrates: 5g, Fat: 8g, Fiber: 1g, Cholesterol: 90mg, Sodium: 300mg, Potassium: 280mg.

Spinach and Feta Stuffed Chicken

 4 servings 20 minutes 25 minutes

Ingredients:

- 4 boneless, skinless chicken breasts
- 2 cups fresh spinach, chopped
- 1/2 cup feta cheese, crumbled
- 2 cloves garlic, minced
- 1 tablespoon olive oil
- Salt and pepper to taste
- 1 teaspoon dried oregano
- Toothpicks or kitchen twine for securing

Directions:

1. Preheat your oven to 375°F (190°C).
2. In a skillet over medium heat, sauté the spinach and garlic in olive oil until the spinach is wilted. Let it cool, then mix in the crumbled feta cheese.
3. Butterfly the chicken breasts (cut them horizontally but not all through) and open them out flat. Season both sides with salt, pepper, and dried oregano.
4. Divide the spinach and feta mixture evenly among the chicken breasts, placing it on one-half of each opened breast. Fold the other half to enclose the filling and secure it with toothpicks or kitchen twine.
5. Place the stuffed chicken breasts in a baking dish and bake in the oven for 25 minutes until the chicken is cooked and no longer pink inside.
6. Let the chicken rest for a few minutes before serving. Remove toothpicks or twine before serving.

This Spinach and Feta Stuffed Chicken recipe offers a delicious and healthy option for a low-cholesterol dinner. The combination of lean chicken, nutrient-rich spinach, and flavorful feta provides a balanced meal with a good source of protein, vitamins, and minerals.

Nutritional Information: (per serving, approximate) Calories: 250, Protein: 35g, Carbohydrates: 3g, Fat: 11g, Fiber: 1g, Cholesterol: 85mg, Sodium: 400mg, Potassium: 450mg.

Chicken Tikka Masala with Cauliflower Rice

 4 servings |  20 minutes | 40 minutes

Ingredients:

- 1 lb chicken breast, cut into chunks
- 1 head of cauliflower, grated into rice-sized pieces
- 1 cup plain low-fat yogurt
- 2 tablespoons olive oil
- 1 large onion, finely chopped
- 3 cloves garlic, minced
- 1 tablespoon grated ginger
- 2 tablespoons tikka masala paste
- 1 can (14 oz) diced tomatoes
- 1 can (14 oz) light coconut milk
- 1 teaspoon turmeric
- Salt and pepper to taste
- Fresh cilantro for garnish

Directions:

- Marinate chicken pieces in yogurt and tikka masala paste in the refrigerator for at least 1 hour.
- Heat 1 tablespoon olive oil in a large skillet over medium heat. Add the marinated chicken and cook until browned on all sides. Remove chicken from skillet and set aside.
- In the same skillet, add another tablespoon of olive oil, onion, garlic, and ginger. Saute until the onion is translucent.
- Add diced tomatoes, coconut milk, and turmeric to the skillet. Bring to a simmer.
- Return the chicken to the skillet, cover, and simmer for 20 minutes.
- While the chicken is cooking, prepare the cauliflower rice by heating it in a separate skillet with a bit of olive oil, salt, and pepper until tender.
- Serve the chicken tikka masala over the cauliflower rice, garnished with fresh cilantro.

This Chicken Tikka Masala with Cauliflower Rice is a delicious low-cholesterol alternative to traditional recipes. Light coconut milk and low-fat yogurt reduce the fat content without sacrificing flavor. Cauliflower rice is a healthy, low-carb substitute for white rice, making this dish perfect for those looking to maintain a balanced diet.

Nutritional Information: (per serving, approximate) Calories: 350, Protein: 28g, Carbohydrates: 15g, Fat: 18g, Fiber: 4g, Cholesterol: 75mg, Sodium: 300mg, Potassium: 800mg.

Roasted Duck Breast
with Pomegranate Glaze and Quinoa Salad

 4 servings | 20 minutes | 25 minutes

Ingredients:

- 4 skinless duck breasts
- Salt and pepper to taste
- 1 cup quinoa
- 2 cups water or chicken broth (low sodium)
- 1/2 cup pomegranate juice
- 2 tablespoons honey
- 1 tablespoon balsamic vinegar
- 4 cups mixed salad greens
- 1/2 cup pomegranate seeds
- 1/4 cup slivered almonds, toasted
- 1/4 cup fresh mint, chopped
- 2 tablespoons olive oil

Directions:

1. Preheat the oven to 375°F (190°C). Season the skinless duck breasts with salt and pepper.
2. Heat a non-stick skillet over medium-high heat. Once hot, add the duck breasts and cook for about 2 minutes on each side to develop a golden color.
3. Transfer the duck breasts to a baking dish and roast in the oven for about 15-20 minutes, or until they reach an internal temperature of 165°F (74°C). Let the duck rest for a few minutes before slicing.
4. While the duck is roasting, rinse quinoa under cold water. In a medium saucepan, bring water or broth to a boil. Add quinoa, reduce heat to low, cover, and simmer for about 15 minutes or until all liquid is absorbed. Fluff with a fork and allow to cool slightly.
5. In a small saucepan, combine pomegranate juice, honey, and balsamic vinegar for the pomegranate glaze. Simmer over medium heat until reduced by half, creating a thick glaze, about 10 minutes.
6. Mix the cooled quinoa with salad greens, pomegranate seeds, almonds, and mint in a large bowl. Drizzle with olive oil and gently toss.
7. Serve sliced duck over the quinoa salad and drizzle with the pomegranate glaze.

Removing the skin from the duck breasts significantly reduces the fat content, especially saturated fat and cholesterol, making this dish suitable for a low-cholesterol diet. The pomegranate glaze and quinoa salad add fresh, tangy, and sweet flavors to complement the rich taste of the duck without the need for its skin, ensuring a delicious and heart-healthy meal.

Nutritional Information: (per serving, approximate) Calories: 400, Protein: 24g, Carbohydrates: 45g, Fat: 14g, Fiber: 6g, Cholesterol: 55mg, Sodium: 220mg, Potassium: 700mg.

Beef Stir-Fry with Bell Peppers and Snow Peas

 **4** servings   **15** minutes   **10** minutes

Ingredients:

- 1 lb lean beef (such as flank steak), thinly sliced against the grain
- 2 bell peppers (any color) sliced into strips
- 1 cup snow peas, trimmed
- 2 tablespoons low-sodium soy sauce
- 1 tablespoon olive oil
- 1 tablespoon fresh ginger, minced
- 2 cloves garlic, minced
- 1 tablespoon honey
- 1 teaspoon cornstarch dissolved in 2 tablespoons water
- Salt and pepper to taste
- Cooked brown rice or quinoa for serving

Directions:

1. Mix soy sauce, honey, and cornstarch in a small bowl. Set aside.
2. Heat olive oil in a large skillet or wok over medium-high heat. Add ginger and garlic, and stir-fry for about 30 seconds or until fragrant.
3. Add the beef slices to the skillet, seasoning with a pinch of salt and pepper. Stir-fry for 2-3 minutes or until the beef is just browned. Remove beef from the skillet and set aside.
4. Add bell peppers and snow peas in the same skillet. Stir-fry for about 2-3 minutes or until vegetables are tender-crisp.
5. Return the beef to the skillet. Pour the soy sauce mixture over the meat and vegetables. Stir well to combine and cook for another 2 minutes until the sauce thickens slightly.
6. Serve the beef stir-fry over cooked brown rice or quinoa.

This Beef Stir-Fry with Bell Peppers and Snow Peas is a vibrant, flavorful dish that keeps things light and healthy. Using lean beef and plenty of fresh vegetables, it's an excellent option for a low-cholesterol diet. The stir-fry pairs beautifully with whole grains like brown rice or quinoa, making it a balanced meal high in protein and fiber while maintaining a low saturated fat and cholesterol level.

Nutritional Information: (per serving, approximate) Calories: 300, Protein: 26g, Carbohydrates: 20g, Fat: 12g, Fiber: 3g, Cholesterol: 50mg, Sodium: 300mg, Potassium: 600mg.

Mediterranean Quinoa Salad

 4 servings | 15 minutes | 15 minutes

Ingredients:

- 1 cup quinoa
- 2 cups water
- 1 cup cherry tomatoes, halved
- 1 cucumber, diced
- 1/2 red onion, finely chopped
- 1/4 cup kalamata olives, pitted and halved
- 1/4 cup feta cheese, crumbled (optional; omit for a vegan option)
- 1/4 cup fresh parsley, chopped
- 2 tablespoons extra virgin olive oil
- Juice of 1 lemon
- Salt and pepper to taste

Directions:

1. Rinse the quinoa in cold water in a fine-mesh strainer to remove bitterness.
2. Bring 2 cups of water to a boil in a medium saucepan. Add the quinoa, reduce heat to low, cover, and simmer for about 15 minutes, until the quinoa is cooked and water is absorbed.
3. Remove the quinoa from heat and let it cool to room temperature. You can also fluff it with a fork and spread it on a baking sheet to cool faster.
4. Combine the cooled quinoa, cherry tomatoes, cucumber, red onion, kalamata olives, and fresh parsley in a large bowl.
5. Drizzle with extra virgin olive oil and lemon juice, then toss to combine. Season with salt and pepper to taste.
6. Gently fold in the feta cheese, if using, just before serving.

With its fresh vegetables, heart-healthy olive oil, and protein-rich quinoa, this salad is delicious and nourishing, making it a great addition to any heart-healthy diet.

Nutritional Information: (per serving, approximate) Calories: 220, Protein: 6 g, Carbohydrates: 35 g, Fat: 7 g, Fiber: 5 g, Cholesterol: 0 mg (without feta) / 5 mg (with feta), Sodium: 150 mg, Potassium: 300 mg

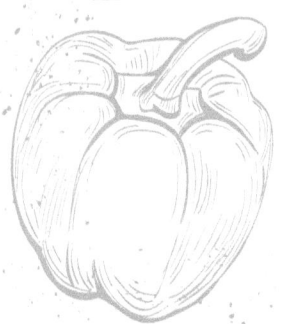

Mediterranean Chickpea Salad

 4 servings   15 minutes 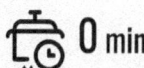 0 minutes

Ingredients:

- 2 cans (15 oz each) chickpeas, drained and rinsed
- 1 cucumber, diced
- 1 red bell pepper, diced
- 1/2 red onion, finely chopped
- 1/4 cup Kalamata olives, pitted and sliced
- 1/4 cup crumbled feta cheese
- 1/4 cup fresh parsley, chopped
- 3 tablespoons olive oil
- 2 tablespoons lemon juice
- 1 teaspoon dried oregano
- Salt and pepper to taste

Directions:

1. Combine the drained and rinsed chickpeas, diced cucumber, red bell pepper, chopped red onion, sliced Kalamata olives, and crumbled feta cheese in a large mixing bowl.
2. Whisk the olive oil, lemon juice, dried oregano, salt, and pepper in a small bowl to create the dressing.
3. Pour the dressing over the chickpea mixture and toss well to ensure all the ingredients are evenly coated.
4. Add the chopped fresh parsley to the salad and mix gently.
5. Taste and adjust the seasoning as needed.
6. The salad can be served immediately or chilled in the refrigerator for 1 hour to allow flavors to meld.
7. Serve as a refreshing side dish or a light main meal.

This Mediterranean Chickpea Salad is a vibrant and nutritious meal perfect for a low-cholesterol diet. Packed with fiber-rich chickpeas and various fresh vegetables, this salad is satisfying and heart-healthy. The tangy lemon dressing and feta cheese add a delicious Mediterranean flair, making it an excellent option for a quick lunch or a healthy side dish.

Nutritional Information: (per serving, approximate) Calories: 330, Protein: 10g, Carbohydrates: 35g, Fat: 17g, Fiber: 10g, Cholesterol: 8mg, Sodium: 300mg, Potassium: 400mg.

Spinach and Strawberry Salad with Balsamic Glaze

 4 servings | 15 minutes | 0 minutes

Ingredients:

- 6 cups fresh baby spinach
- 2 cups strawberries, sliced
- 1/2 cup walnut halves, toasted
- 1/4 cup crumbled goat cheese
- 1/4 cup red onion, thinly sliced

For the Balsamic Glaze:

- 1/2 cup balsamic vinegar
- 2 tablespoons honey

Directions:

1. In a small saucepan, combine balsamic vinegar and honey. Bring to a simmer over medium heat and cook until the mixture is reduced by half and becomes syrupy, about 10 minutes. Set aside to cool.
2. Combine the fresh baby spinach, sliced strawberries, toasted walnut halves, crumbled goat cheese, and thinly sliced red onion in a large salad bowl.
3. Drizzle the balsamic glaze over the salad just before serving.
4. Toss the salad gently to combine all the ingredients and coat them with the glaze.
5. Serve immediately for the freshest taste.

This Spinach and Strawberry Salad with Balsamic Glaze is a delightful blend of sweet and tangy flavors combined with the richness of goat cheese and the crunch of toasted walnuts. The homemade balsamic glaze adds a gourmet touch to this simple yet elegant salad, making it a perfect choice for a low-cholesterol diet. It's not only delicious but also packed with antioxidants and nutrients.

Nutritional Information: (per serving, approximate) Calories: 180, Protein: 6g, Carbohydrates: 20g, Fat: 10g, Fiber: 4g, Cholesterol: 6mg, Sodium: 80mg, Potassium: 450mg.

Grilled Chicken and Mango Salad

 4 servings | **20** minutes | **10** minutes

Ingredients:

- 2 boneless, skinless chicken breasts
- Salt and pepper to taste
- 1 tablespoon olive oil
- 1 large ripe mango, peeled and sliced
- 6 cups mixed salad greens (e.g., lettuce, spinach, arugula)
- 1/2 red bell pepper, thinly sliced
- 1/4 red onion, thinly sliced
- 1/4 cup fresh cilantro, chopped

For the Dressing:

- 3 tablespoons lime juice
- 2 tablespoons olive oil
- 1 tablespoon honey
- 1 teaspoon Dijon mustard
- Salt and pepper to taste

Directions:

1. Preheat the grill to medium-high heat. Brush the chicken breasts with olive oil and season with salt and pepper.
2. Grill the chicken for 5 minutes on each side until fully cooked and no longer pink inside. Remove from the grill and let it rest for a few minutes before slicing.
3. Combine the mixed salad greens, sliced mango, red bell pepper, red onion, and chopped cilantro in a large bowl.
4. In a small bowl, whisk together lime juice, olive oil, honey, Dijon mustard, salt, and pepper to make the dressing.
5. Add the grilled chicken slices to the salad.
6. Drizzle the dressing over the salad and toss gently to combine.
7. Serve immediately, ensuring each serving has a good mix of salad greens, mango, vegetables, and grilled chicken.

This Grilled Chicken and Mango Salad is a light and refreshing dish combining mango sweetness with grilled chicken's savory flavor. The homemade lime dressing adds a zesty and slightly sweet touch, making it a perfect meal for a low-cholesterol diet. It's an excellent source of protein and vitamins, and the colorful presentation makes it as appealing to the eye as it is to the palate.

Nutritional Information: (per serving, approximate) Calories: 250, Protein: 18g, Carbohydrates: 20g, Fat: 11g, Fiber: 3g, Cholesterol: 40mg, Sodium: 150mg, Potassium: 500mg.

Arugula and Pear Salad with Lemon Dressing

 **4** servings | **15** minutes | **0** minutes

Ingredients:

• 5 cups arugula leaves, washed and dried
• 2 ripe pears, cored and thinly sliced
• 1/4 cup shaved Parmesan cheese (you can substitute with feta cheese or goat cheese)
• 1/4 cup toasted walnuts, chopped

For the Lemon Dressing:

• 3 tablespoons extra-virgin olive oil
• 2 tablespoons fresh lemon juice
• 1 teaspoon honey
• 1 small garlic clove, minced
• Salt and pepper to taste

Directions:

1. Whisk the extra-virgin olive oil, fresh lemon juice, honey, minced garlic, salt, and pepper to create the lemon dressing in a small bowl. Set aside.
2. Combine the arugula leaves and thinly sliced pears in a large salad bowl.
3. Drizzle the lemon dressing over the salad and toss gently to coat the arugula and pears evenly.
4. Add the shaved Parmesan cheese and toasted walnuts to the salad.
5. Toss the salad lightly once more to distribute the cheese and nuts.
6. Serve the salad immediately to enjoy the fresh and crisp flavors.
7. Optional: To add protein, topping the salad with grilled chicken or salmon.

This Arugula and Pear Salad with Lemon Dressing is a delightful combination of peppery arugula, sweet pears, and a tangy lemon dressing. Adding shaved Parmesan and toasted walnuts gives depth and richness, making it a satisfying yet light choice for a low-cholesterol diet. The salad is simple to prepare and perfect as a starter or a light meal.

Nutritional Information: (per serving, approximate) Calories: 180, Protein: 5g, Carbohydrates: 12g, Fat: 14g, Fiber: 3g, Cholesterol: 4mg, Sodium: 150mg, Potassium: 250mg.

Lentil and Roasted Red Pepper Salad

🍽 4 servings | ⏰ 20 minutes | ⏲ 25 minutes

Ingredients:

- 1 cup dry green lentils
- 2 cups water
- 2 roasted red peppers, diced
- 1/2 red onion, finely chopped
- 1/4 cup fresh parsley, chopped
- 1/4 cup crumbled feta cheese
- 3 tablespoons olive oil
- 2 tablespoons red wine vinegar
- 1 garlic clove, minced
- Salt and pepper to taste

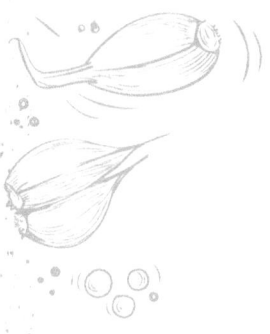

Directions:

1. Rinse the lentils and add them to a pot with 2 cups of water. Bring to a boil, then reduce heat and simmer for about 20-25 minutes, until lentils are tender but firm.
2. Drain the lentils and let them cool.
3. Combine the cooled lentils, diced roasted red peppers, chopped red onion, and fresh parsley in a large bowl.
4. Whisk olive oil, red wine vinegar, minced garlic, salt, and pepper in a small bowl to create the dressing.
5. Pour the dressing over the lentil mixture and toss to coat evenly.
6. Gently fold in the crumbled feta cheese.
7. Adjust seasoning with additional salt and pepper if needed.
8. Serve the salad chilled or at room temperature.

This Lentil and Roasted Red Pepper Salad is hearty and nutritious, perfect for a low-cholesterol diet. The lentils provide an excellent plant-based protein and fiber source, while the roasted red peppers add a sweet and smoky flavor. The addition of feta cheese offers a tangy contrast and complements the overall taste. It's an excellent choice for a healthy lunch or as a side dish.

Nutritional Information: (per serving, approximate) Calories: 290, Protein: 14g, Carbohydrates: 33g, Fat: 12g, Fiber: 9g, Cholesterol: 8mg, Sodium: 200mg, Potassium: 470mg.

Tuna and White Bean Salad
with Lemon Vinaigrette

Ingredients:

- 2 cans (5 ounces each) of tuna in water, drained and flaked
- 1 can (15 ounces) white beans, rinsed and drained
- 1/2 red onion, thinly sliced
- 1/2 cup cherry tomatoes, halved
- 1/4 cup chopped fresh parsley
- 1/4 cup extra-virgin olive oil
- 2 tablespoons fresh lemon juice
- 1 garlic clove, minced
- Salt and pepper to taste
- Lemon zest for garnish

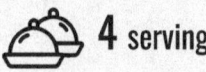 4 servings |  15 minutes | 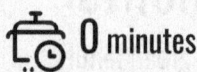 0 minutes

Directions:

1. Combine the flaked tuna, white beans, sliced red onion, halved cherry tomatoes, and chopped fresh parsley in a large bowl.
2. Whisk the extra-virgin olive oil, fresh lemon juice, minced garlic, salt, and pepper to create the lemon vinaigrette in a small bowl.
3. Pour the vinaigrette over the tuna and bean mixture. Toss gently to coat all the ingredients evenly.
4. Let the salad sit for a few minutes to allow the flavors to meld together.
5. Garnish with lemon zest right before serving.
6. Adjust the seasoning with additional salt and pepper if needed.
7. Serve chilled or at room temperature as a light meal or a healthy side dish.

This Tuna and White Bean Salad with Lemon Vinaigrette is a refreshing, protein-packed dish for a low-cholesterol diet. The combination of tuna and beans provides a satisfying texture and plenty of heart-healthy nutrients. The zesty lemon vinaigrette adds a bright and tangy flavor, making this salad a delightful option for a quick lunch or a nutritious addition to any meal.

Nutritional Information: (per serving, approximate) Calories: 280, Protein: 23g, Carbohydrates: 22g, Fat: 12g, Fiber: 6g, Cholesterol: 30mg, Sodium: 300mg, Potassium: 480mg.

Shrimp and Avocado Salad with Citrus Dressing

Ingredients:

- 1 pound cooked shrimp, peeled and deveined
- 2 ripe avocados, diced
- 1/2 red onion, thinly sliced
- 1/2 cup cherry tomatoes, halved
- 1/4 cup fresh cilantro, chopped
- 1/4 cup orange juice
- 2 tablespoons lime juice
- 1 tablespoon olive oil
- 1 garlic clove, minced
- Salt and pepper to taste
- Orange and lime zest for garnish

 4 servings 20 minutes 5 minutes

Directions:

1. Combine the cooked shrimp, diced avocados, sliced red onion, halved cherry tomatoes, and chopped cilantro in a large bowl.
2. Whisk the orange juice, lime juice, olive oil, minced garlic, salt, and pepper to create the citrus dressing in a small bowl.
3. Pour the dressing over the shrimp and avocado mixture. Toss gently to coat all the ingredients evenly.
4. Let the salad sit for a few minutes to allow the flavors to meld together.
5. Garnish with orange and lime zest right before serving.
6. Adjust the seasoning with additional salt and pepper if needed.
7. Serve chilled as a refreshing and nutritious meal.

This Shrimp and Avocado Salad with Citrus Dressing is a vibrant and healthy choice for those following a low-cholesterol diet. The combination of succulent shrimp and creamy avocado provides an excellent source of protein and heart-healthy fats. The citrus dressing adds a bright and zesty flavor, complementing the fresh ingredients perfectly. This salad is delicious and packed with nutrients, making it a great option for a light lunch or as part of a balanced meal.

Nutritional Information: (per serving, approximate) Calories: 250, Protein: 24g, Carbohydrates: 12g, Fat: 12g, Fiber: 6g, Cholesterol: 180mg, Sodium: 300mg, Potassium: 450mg.

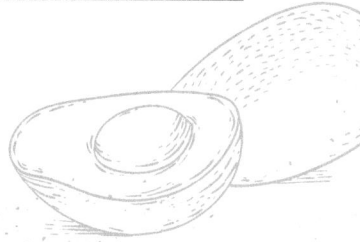

Tomato, Basil and Mozzarella Caprese Salad

 **4 servings** **10 minutes**  **0 minutes**

Ingredients:

- 4 large ripe tomatoes, sliced
- 8 ounces fresh mozzarella cheese, sliced
- 1/4 cup fresh basil leaves
- 2 tablespoons extra-virgin olive oil
- 1 tablespoon balsamic vinegar
- Salt and pepper to taste

Directions:

1. Arrange the tomato and mozzarella slices on a platter, alternating and overlapping them.
2. Tuck whole basil leaves between the slices of tomato and mozzarella.
3. Drizzle the olive oil and balsamic vinegar over the arranged slices.
4. Sprinkle salt and pepper to taste.
5. Let the salad sit for 5-10 minutes to allow the flavors to meld.
6. Serve as a refreshing and colorful starter or side dish.

This Tomato, Basil, and Mozzarella Caprese Salad is a classic Italian meal that is simple yet flavorful. A light dressing of olive oil and balsamic vinegar enhances the combination of juicy tomatoes, creamy mozzarella, and fresh basil. It's a delightful salad that's both refreshing and satisfying, making it the right choice for a low-cholesterol diet. Enjoy this traditional Caprese salad's vibrant colors and flavors as a healthy appetizer or side.

Nutritional Information: (per serving, approximate) Calories: 220, Protein: 14g, Carbohydrates: 6g, Fat: 16g, Fiber: 2g, Cholesterol: 45mg, Sodium: 280mg, Potassium: 300mg.

Broccoli and Almond Salad with Yogurt Dressing

 **4 servings** **15 minutes** 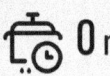 **0 minutes**

Ingredients:

- 4 cups broccoli florets, raw or lightly steamed
- 1/2 cup slivered almonds, toasted
- 1/4 cup red onion, finely chopped
- 1/2 cup plain low-fat yogurt
- 2 tablespoons lemon juice
- 1 tablespoon honey
- 1 garlic clove, minced
- Salt and pepper to taste
- Optional: 1/4 cup dried cranberries or raisins for added sweetness

Directions:

1. Combine the broccoli florets, slivered almonds, and red onion in a large bowl.
2. In a small bowl, whisk together the yogurt, lemon juice, honey, minced garlic, salt, and pepper to create the dressing.
3. Pour the dressing over the broccoli mixture and toss until well-coated.
4. If desired, add dried cranberries or raisins and mix gently.
5. Let the salad chill in the refrigerator for at least 30 minutes to allow the flavors to meld.
6. Serve chilled as a refreshing and healthy side dish.
7. Enjoy a nutrient-rich salad that's perfect for a low-cholesterol diet.

This low-cholesterol salad is packed with nutrients and flavor and offers a delightful texture contrast, making it a healthy and satisfying addition to any meal.

Nutritional Information: (per serving, approximate) Calories: 150, Protein: 6g, Carbohydrates: 15g, Fat: 9g, Fiber: 4g, Cholesterol: 3mg, Sodium: 70mg, Potassium: 360mg.

Poached Salmon Salad with Dill and Cucumber

Ingredients:

 4 servings | 15minutes | 10 minutes

- 4 salmon fillets (4 oz each)
- 1 large cucumber, thinly sliced
- 2 tablespoons fresh dill, chopped
- 8 cups mixed salad greens
- 1/4 cup red onion, thinly sliced
- Lemon wedges for serving

Directions:

1. Bring a large pot of water to a gentle simmer. Add the salmon fillets and poach for about 8-10 minutes or until cooked. Remove from the water and let cool.
2. Flake the poached salmon into large pieces, discarding the skin.
3. In a small bowl, whisk together the Greek yogurt, lemon juice, olive oil, minced garlic, salt, and pepper to make the dressing.
4. Combine the mixed salad greens, cucumber slices, red onion, and chopped dill in a large bowl.
5. Add the flaked salmon to the salad.
6. Drizzle the dressing over the salad and gently toss to combine.
7. Serve the salad with lemon wedges on the side.

For the Dressing:

- 1/4 cup low-fat Greek yogurt
- 2 tablespoons fresh lemon juice
- 1 tablespoon olive oil
- 1 garlic clove, minced
- Salt and pepper to taste

This Poached Salmon Salad with Dill and Cucumber is a light, refreshing meal perfect for a low-cholesterol diet. Enjoy this nutritious salad for a satisfying lunch or a light dinner.

Nutritional Information: (per serving, approximate) Calories: 280, Protein: 28g, Carbohydrates: 10g, Fat: 15g, Fiber: 3g, Cholesterol: 60mg, Sodium: 200mg, Potassium: 750mg.

Turkey and Cranberry Spinach Salad

Ingredients:

- 8 cups fresh spinach leaves, washed and dried
- 1 cup cooked turkey breast, shredded or sliced
- 1/2 cup dried cranberries
- 1/2 cup chopped walnuts
- 1/4 cup red onion, thinly sliced
- 1/4 cup crumbled feta cheese
- 3 tablespoons olive oil
- 1 tablespoon apple cider vinegar
- 1 teaspoon honey
- 1 teaspoon Dijon mustard
- Salt and pepper to taste

 4 servings  15 minutes 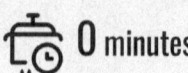 0 minutes

Directions:

1. Combine spinach, turkey, cranberries, walnuts, red onion, and feta cheese in a large bowl.
2. Whisk olive oil, apple cider vinegar, honey, Dijon mustard, salt, and pepper in a small bowl to create the dressing.
3. Drizzle the dressing over the salad and toss gently to combine.
4. Let the salad sit for a few minutes for flavors to meld.
5. Serve the salad on individual plates or in a large sharing bowl.
6. Enjoy a healthy and delicious meal, perfect for a low-cholesterol diet.

This salad is an excellent choice for a light lunch or a side dish, offering a good source of protein and fiber with low cholesterol content.

Nutritional Information: (per serving, approximate) Calories: 280, Protein: 18g, Carbohydrates: 22g, Fat: 16g, Fiber: 4g, Cholesterol: 30mg, Sodium: 250mg, Potassium: 480mg.

Pear and Walnut Salad with Blue Cheese

Ingredients:

- 2 ripe pears, cored and thinly sliced
- 6 cups mixed greens (e.g., arugula, spinach, lettuce)
- 1/2 cup walnuts, toasted and chopped
- 1/4 cup crumbled blue cheese (low-fat, if available)
- 2 tablespoons extra virgin olive oil
- 2 tablespoons balsamic vinegar
- 1 teaspoon Dijon mustard
- 1 teaspoon honey
- Salt and pepper to taste

 4 servings 15 minutes 0 minutes

Directions:

1. Combine the mixed greens and sliced pears in a large salad bowl.
2. In a small dry skillet over medium heat, toast the walnuts until fragrant, about 3-4 minutes. Let cool, and then chop.
3. Sprinkle the toasted walnuts and crumbled blue cheese over the salad.
4. In a small bowl, whisk together the olive oil, balsamic vinegar, Dijon mustard, honey, salt, and pepper to create the dressing.
5. Drizzle the dressing over the salad and toss gently to coat.
6. Serve immediately, optionally garnished with additional blue cheese or walnuts.

This salad balances the sweetness of pears with the tangy taste of blue cheese and the crunch of walnuts, making it a delightful and nutritious choice for those following a low-cholesterol diet.

Nutritional Information: (per serving, approximate) Calories: 210, Protein: 5g, Carbohydrates: 17g, Fat: 15g, Fiber: 3g, Cholesterol: 8mg, Sodium: 190mg, Potassium: 300mg.

Crispy Tofu and Noodle Salad

Ingredients:

 4 servings | **15**minutes | **15** minutes

- 14 ounces firm tofu, drained and cut into cubes
- 2 tablespoons olive oil
- 8 ounces rice noodles
- 1 medium carrot, julienned
- 1 red bell pepper, thinly sliced
- 1 cucumber, thinly sliced
- 1/4 cup fresh cilantro, chopped (optional)
- 1/4 cup fresh mint, chopped (optional)
- 2 green onions, thinly sliced
- 2 tablespoons low-sodium soy sauce
- 1 tablespoon rice vinegar
- 1 tablespoon lime juice
- 1 tablespoon honey
- 1 teaspoon sesame oil
- 1 clove garlic, minced
- Crushed red pepper flakes, to taste (optional)

Directions:

1. Press tofu between paper towels to remove excess moisture.
2. Heat olive oil in a pan over medium heat. Add tofu and cook until crispy, about 5 minutes per side.
3. Cook rice noodles according to package instructions. Rinse under cold water and drain.
4. Combine cooked noodles, carrot, bell pepper, cucumber, cilantro, mint, and green onions in a large bowl.
5. Whisk soy sauce, rice vinegar, lime juice, honey, sesame oil, garlic, and red pepper flakes in a small bowl.
6. Add crispy tofu to the salad. Pour dressing over the salad and toss gently to combine.
7. Serve immediately or refrigerate until ready to eat.

Crispy Tofu and Noodle Salad is a delightful and light meal that combines the satisfying crunch of pan-fried tofu with the noodles' soft texture. All tossed together with a vibrant mix of fresh vegetables and a flavorful dressing. This dish is perfect for those seeking a nutritious, low-cholesterol option that doesn't compromise taste or texture.

Nutritional Information (per serving, approximate): Calories: 360, Protein: 16g, Carbohydrates: 48g, Fat: 12g, Fiber: 2g, Cholesterol: 0mg, Sodium: 300mg, Potassium: 200mg.

Spinach, Avocado, and Pomegranate Salad

Ingredients:

- 6 cups fresh spinach leaves, washed and dried
- 1 ripe avocado, diced
- 1/2 cup pomegranate arils
- 1/4 cup red onion, thinly sliced
- 1/4 cup walnuts, chopped
- 2 tablespoons extra-virgin olive oil
- 2 tablespoons balsamic vinegar
- 1 teaspoon Dijon mustard
- 1 teaspoon honey
- Salt and pepper, to taste

 4 servings | 10 minutes | 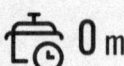 0 minutes

Directions:

1. Combine spinach, avocado, pomegranate arils, red onion, and walnuts in a large salad bowl.
2. Whisk olive oil, balsamic vinegar, Dijon mustard, honey, salt, and pepper in a small bowl.
3. Drizzle the dressing over the salad and toss gently to coat.
4. Adjust seasoning with additional salt and pepper if needed.
5. Serve immediately for the freshest taste.

Spinach, Avocado, and Pomegranate Salad is a vibrant and nutrient-rich dish that combines tender spinach leaves, creamy avocado slices, and juicy pomegranate seeds. This low-cholesterol salad is dressed in a light, flavorful vinaigrette, making it a perfect choice for those seeking a heart-healthy, delicious, easy-to-prepare meal.

Nutritional Information (per serving, approximate): Calories: 230, Protein: 4g, Carbohydrates: 14g, Fat: 19g, Fiber: 6g, Cholesterol: 0mg, Sodium: 60mg, Potassium: 450mg.

Cucumber Sesame Salad

Ingredients:

- 2 large cucumbers
- 2 tablespoons rice vinegar
- 1 tablespoon soy sauce (low sodium)
- 1 teaspoon sugar
- 1 teaspoon sesame oil
- 2 tablespoons sesame seeds, toasted
- A pinch of red pepper flakes (optional)

This Cucumber Sesame Salad is a light, healthy side dish perfect for a low-cholesterol diet. It combines the crisp freshness of cucumber with the rich flavors of sesame and a hint of sweetness and heat, making it an ideal complement to any main course.

 4 servings | 10 minutes | 10 minutes

Directions:

1. Wash the cucumbers and slice them thinly. You can use a mandoline slicer to make uniform, thin slices.
2. In a small bowl, mix rice vinegar, low-sodium soy sauce, sugar, and sesame oil until the sugar dissolves.
3. Place the cucumber slices in a large bowl, pour the dressing over them, and gently toss to coat evenly.
4. Sprinkle the toasted sesame seeds over the cucumbers, and add a pinch of red pepper flakes if you like a bit of heat.
5. Let the salad sit for about 10 minutes to marinate and absorb the flavors before serving.
6. Serve the salad chilled or at room temperature.
7. Enjoy this refreshing side dish that complements any meal, especially those with a low-cholesterol focus.

Nutritional Information: (per serving, approximate) Calories: 70, Protein: 2 g, Carbohydrates: 8 g, Fat: 4 g, Fiber: 1 g, Cholesterol: 0 mg, Sodium: 150 mg, Potassium: 200 mg

Grilled Chicken, Avocado and Mixed Greens Salad

 4 servings |  15 minutes |  10 minutes

Ingredients:

- 2 medium chicken breasts, boneless and skinless
- 1 large avocado, diced
- 4 cups mixed greens (arugula, spinach, romaine)
- 1 cup cherry tomatoes, halved
- 1/2 cup cucumber, diced
- 1/4 cup red onion, thinly sliced
- 2 tablespoons extra virgin olive oil, plus more for grilling
- Juice of 1 lemon
- Salt and pepper to taste
- Optional: 1/4 cup crumbled feta cheese (omit for strict low-cholesterol diets)

Directions:

1. Preheat the grill to medium-high heat. Brush chicken breasts with olive oil and season with salt and pepper.
2. Grill chicken for 5 minutes on each side or until fully cooked (internal temperature of 165°F). Let it rest for a few minutes, then slice thinly.
3. Combine mixed greens, cherry tomatoes, cucumber, and red onion in a large salad bowl.
4. Add the diced avocado to the salad.
5. In a small bowl, whisk together two tablespoons of olive oil, lemon juice, salt, and pepper to create the dressing.
6. Add the grilled chicken slices to the salad. Drizzle the dressing over the salad and toss gently to combine.
7. Serve immediately, optionally topped with crumbled feta cheese.

This Grilled Chicken, Avocado, and Mixed Greens Salad is a heart-healthy, low-cholesterol dish that combines lean protein, healthy fats, and fresh vegetables in a flavorful and nutritious meal. Perfect for a light lunch or as a side salad for dinner, this recipe is both satisfying and aligned with a low-cholesterol dietary approach.

Nutritional Information (per serving, approximate): Calories: 290, Protein: 26 g, Carbohydrates: 12 g, Fat: 16 g, Fiber: 6 g, Cholesterol: 65 mg, Sodium: 200 mg, Potassium: 700 mg

Salad with Lemon-Olive Dressing

 4 servings  10 minutes  10 minutes

Ingredients:

For the Salad:

- 6 cups mixed salad greens (such as spinach, arugula, and romaine)
- 1 cucumber, thinly sliced
- 1 cup cherry tomatoes, halved
- 1/4 cup sliced red onion
- 1/4 cup sliced black olives
- 2 tablespoons chopped fresh parsley (optional)
- Salt and black pepper to taste

For the Lemon-Olive Dressing:

- 1/4 cup extra-virgin olive oil
- 2 tablespoons freshly squeezed lemon juice
- 1 teaspoon Dijon mustard
- 1 clove garlic, minced
- 1 teaspoon honey (optional)
- Salt and black pepper to taste

Directions:

1. In a large salad bowl, combine the mixed salad greens, thinly sliced cucumber, halved cherry tomatoes, sliced red onion, sliced black olives, and chopped fresh parsley (if using). Season with salt and black pepper to taste.
2. In a small mixing bowl, whisk the extra-virgin olive oil, freshly squeezed lemon juice, Dijon mustard, minced garlic, honey (if using), salt, and black pepper until well combined.
3. Drizzle the Lemon-Olive Dressing over the salad mixture in the bowl.
4. Toss the salad gently to coat all the ingredients evenly with the dressing.
5. Taste the salad and adjust the seasoning or add more dressing if needed.

Serve the Low-Cholesterol Green Salad with Lemon-Olive Dressing immediately as a refreshing and nutritious side dish or starter.

Nutritional Information: (per serving, approximate) Calories: 120, Protein: 2g, Carbohydrates: 8g, Fat: 10g, Fiber: 3g, Cholesterol: 0mg, Sodium: 150mg, Potassium: 300mg.

Fresh Vegetable Salad with Dijon Dressing

Ingredients:

- Mixed greens (arugula, spinach, lettuce leaves) - 4 cups
- Cucumber, thinly sliced - 1 medium
- Radishes, thinly sliced - 5 to 6
- Cherry tomatoes, halved - 1/2 cup
- Red onion, thinly sliced - 1/4 cup
- For Dijon Dressing:
- Extra virgin olive oil - 3 tablespoons
- Vinegar (wine or apple cider) - 1 tablespoon
- Dijon mustard - 1 teaspoon
- Salt and pepper to taste

 4 servings |  15 minutes |  0 minutes

Directions:

1. Combine the mixed greens, sliced cucumber, radishes, cherry tomatoes, and red onion in a large salad bowl.
2. In a small bowl, whisk the extra virgin olive oil, vinegar, Dijon mustard, salt, and pepper to make the dressing.
3. Drizzle the dressing over the salad ingredients and gently toss to coat evenly.
4. Serve the salad immediately or chill in the refrigerator for 30 minutes to enhance the flavors.
5. Enjoy as a refreshing side to any main course.

This Fresh Vegetable Salad with Dijon Dressing is a light, heart-healthy option that perfectly complements a low-cholesterol diet. The crisp vegetables paired with the tangy Dijon dressing offer a delicious way to enjoy a variety of nutrients while keeping your meal balanced and flavorful.

Nutritional Information (per serving, approximate): Calories: 120, Protein: 2g, Carbohydrates: 6g, Fat: 10g, Fiber: 2g, Cholesterol: 0mg, Sodium: 150mg, Potassium: 350mg.

Mediterranean Farro Salad

Ingredients:

- 1 cup farro, rinsed
- 2 cups water or vegetable broth
- 1 cup cherry tomatoes, halved
- 1 cucumber, diced
- 1/2 red onion, finely chopped
- 1/3 cup kalamata olives, pitted and halved
- 1/2 cup feta cheese, crumbled
- 1/4 cup fresh parsley, chopped
- 1/4 cup fresh mint, chopped
- 3 tablespoons extra virgin olive oil
- 2 tablespoons lemon juice
- Salt and pepper to taste

 4 servings |  15 minutes | 30 minutes

Directions:

1. Bring water or vegetable broth to a boil in a medium saucepan. Add farro, reduce heat to low, cover, and simmer for about 30 minutes until farro is tender and liquid is absorbed.
2. Drain any excess liquid from farro and let it cool to room temperature.
3. Combine cooled farro, cherry tomatoes, cucumber, red onion, kalamata olives, feta cheese, parsley, and mint in a large salad bowl.
4. Whisk extra virgin olive oil, lemon juice, salt, and pepper in a small bowl to make the dressing.
5. Pour the dressing over the salad and toss gently to combine and coat evenly.
6. Add salt, pepper or lemon juice if necessary.
7. Serve at room temperature or chilled.

This Mediterranean Farro Salad is a hearty, nutritious dish perfect for a low-cholesterol diet. It combines whole grains, fresh vegetables, and healthy fats to create a delicious and satisfying meal.

Nutritional Information (per serving, approximate): Calories: 300, Protein: 9g, Carbohydrates: 40g, Fat: 12g, Fiber: 8g, Cholesterol: 15mg, Sodium: 200mg, Potassium: 250mg.

Grilled Chicken with Quinoa and Spinach Salad

Ingredients:

4 servings | 20 minutes | 20 minutes

- 4 boneless, skinless chicken breasts
- 1 cup quinoa
- 2 cups water or low-sodium chicken broth
- 4 cups fresh spinach leaves
- 1/2 cup cherry tomatoes, halved
- 1/4 cup red onion, thinly sliced
- 1/4 cup cucumber, sliced
- 2 tablespoons olive oil
- 2 tablespoons balsamic vinegar
- Juice of 1 lemon
- Salt and pepper to taste
- Optional: feta cheese or avocado slices for garnish

Directions:

1. Rinse quinoa under cold water. In a medium saucepan, bring water or broth to a boil. Add quinoa, reduce heat to low, cover, and simmer for 15-20 minutes until water is absorbed. Fluff with a fork and set aside to cool.
2. Preheat the grill to medium-high heat. Season chicken breasts with salt and pepper. Grill 6-7 minutes per side until fully cooked (internal temperature reaches 165°F). Let rest for a few minutes, then slice.
3. Combine cooked quinoa, spinach, cherry tomatoes, red onion, and cucumber in a large bowl. Whisk olive oil, balsamic vinegar, and lemon juice in a small bowl. Pour over salad and toss to coat.
4. Divide salad among plates. Top with sliced grilled chicken. Garnish with feta cheese or avocado slices if desired.

This Grilled Chicken with Quinoa and Spinach Salad is a hearty, nutritious meal perfect for a low-cholesterol diet. It combines lean protein, whole grains, and fresh vegetables, dressed with a simple, heart-healthy vinaigrette.

Nutritional Information (per serving, approximate): Calories: 350, Protein: 30g, Carbohydrates: 35g, Fat: 10g, Fiber: 5g, Cholesterol: 65mg, Sodium: 200mg, Potassium: 700mg.

Cauliflower Steak with Herb Sauce

Ingredients:

- 1 large head cauliflower
- 2 tablespoons olive oil
- 1/2 teaspoon garlic powder
- 1/2 teaspoon smoked paprika
- Salt and pepper, to taste

For the Herb Sauce:

- 1/2 cup fresh parsley, finely chopped
- 1/4 cup fresh basil, finely chopped
- 2 tablespoons olive oil
- 2 tablespoons lemon juice
- 1 garlic clove, minced
- Salt and pepper, to taste

 4 servings 10 minutes 25 minutes

Directions:

1. Preheat oven to 400°F (200°C).
2. Remove the cauliflower leaves and cut them into 1-inch thick slices.
3. Brush each cauliflower steak with olive oil and season with garlic powder, smoked paprika, salt, and pepper.
4. Place cauliflower steaks on a baking sheet and roast for 25 minutes, flipping halfway through, until tender and golden.
5. In a small bowl, prepare the herb sauce by combining parsley, basil, olive oil, lemon juice, garlic, salt, and pepper.
6. Serve the roasted cauliflower steaks with the herb sauce drizzled on top.

This low-cholesterol recipe offers a delightful blend of textures and flavors, making it an ideal choice for anyone looking to enjoy a plant-based, nutritious meal that's both satisfying and heart-healthy.

Nutritional Information: (per serving, approximate) Calories:140, Protein: 3g, Carbohydrates:10g, Fat: 10g, Fiber: 4g, Cholesterol: 0mg, Sodium: 65mg, Potassium: 430mg.

Creamy Avocado Pasta with Cherry Tomatoes and Spinach

Ingredients:

- 8 oz whole wheat pasta
- 1 ripe avocado
- 2 cups cherry tomatoes, halved
- 3 cups fresh spinach
- 2 cloves garlic, minced
- 1 tablespoon lemon juice
- 1/4 cup fresh basil, chopped
- 2 tablespoons olive oil
- Salt and pepper to taste

This low-cholesterol pasta dish is visually appealing and packed with heart-healthy fats and flavors, making it a perfect meal for those seeking a delicious and wholesome dining experience.

 4 servings 15 minutes 10 minutes

Directions:

1. Cook the pasta according to package instructions until al dente. Drain and set aside.
2. Blend the avocado, garlic, lemon juice, and basil until smooth in a food processor.
3. Heat the olive oil in a large skillet over medium heat. Add the cherry tomatoes and cook for 2-3 minutes.
4. Add the spinach to the skillet and cook until just wilted.
5. Add the cooked pasta to the skillet with the tomatoes and spinach.
6. Pour the avocado sauce over the pasta and gently toss to combine.
7. Season with salt and pepper. Serve warm, garnished with additional basil if desired.

Nutritional Information: (per serving, approximate) Calories:330, Protein: 10g, Carbohydrates:49g, Fat: 12g, Fiber: 8g, Cholesterol: 0mg, Sodium: 30mg, Potassium: 450mg.

Vegan Jambalaya with Smoked Paprika

 4 servings  10 minutes  30 minutes

Ingredients:

- 1 tablespoon olive oil
- 1 large onion, diced
- 1 red bell pepper, diced
- 2 celery stalks, diced
- 3 cloves garlic, minced
- 1 cup long-grain brown rice
- 1 can (14.5 oz) diced tomatoes with juice
- 2 cups low-sodium vegetable broth
- 1 cup frozen okra, sliced
- 1 cup canned kidney beans, drained and rinsed
- 1 tablespoon smoked paprika
- 1 teaspoon dried thyme
- 1 teaspoon dried oregano
- 1/2 teaspoon cayenne pepper (adjust to taste)
- Salt and pepper to taste
- Fresh parsley, chopped, for garnish

Directions:

1. Heat the olive oil in a large skillet over medium heat. Add the onion, bell pepper, and celery, and saute for about 5 minutes until softened.
2. Add the garlic and cook for another minute.
3. Stir in the rice, diced tomatoes with juice, vegetable broth, okra, kidney beans, smoked paprika, thyme, oregano, and cayenne pepper. Bring to a boil.
4. Reduce heat to low, cover, and simmer for 20-25 minutes until the rice is cooked and most liquid is absorbed.
5. Season with salt and pepper. Garnish with chopped parsley before serving.

Vegan Jambalaya with Smoked Paprika is a bold and flavorful take on the classic Southern dish, packed with various vegetables and seasoned with smoked paprika for an added depth of flavor. This low-cholesterol version offers a hearty and satisfying meal without animal products, making it ideal for anyone looking to enjoy the rich tastes of jambalaya in a plant-based, heart-healthy form.

Nutritional Information: (per serving, approximate) Calories: 320, Protein: 9g, Carbohydrates: 60g, Fat: 4g, Fiber: 8g, Cholesterol: 0mg, Sodium: 300mg, Potassium: 600mg.

Lentil Loaf with Tomato Glaze

 **6** servings | **15** minutes | **60** minutes

Ingredients:

- 1 cup dried green lentils, rinsed
- 2 cups water
- 1 tablespoon olive oil
- 1 medium onion, finely chopped
- 2 cloves garlic, minced
- 1 medium carrot, grated
- 1/2 cup walnuts, finely chopped
- 1/2 cup rolled oats
- 2 tablespoons ground flaxseed mixed with 6 tablespoons water (flax egg)
- 2 tablespoons soy sauce or tamari
- 1 teaspoon dried thyme
- 1/2 teaspoon smoked paprika
- Salt and pepper to taste
- 1/2 cup ketchup
- 2 tablespoons balsamic vinegar
- 1 tablespoon brown sugar

Directions:

1. Preheat the oven to 350°F (175°C). Lightly grease a loaf pan.
2. In a medium saucepan, combine lentils and water. Bring to a boil, then reduce heat, cover, and simmer for about 20 minutes until lentils are tender. Drain any excess water.
3. Heat olive oil in a skillet over medium heat. Sauté onion, garlic, and carrot until softened, about 5 minutes.
4. Mix cooked lentils, sautéed vegetables, walnuts, oats, flax egg, soy sauce, thyme, smoked paprika, salt, and pepper in a large bowl. Mash some of the lentils with a fork for a better texture.
5. Press the mixture into the prepared loaf pan.
6. Combine ketchup, balsamic vinegar, and brown sugar in a small bowl. Spread this glaze over the top of the lentil loaf.
7. Bake for 40 minutes until the loaf is firm and the glaze is caramelized.
8. Let the lentil loaf cool in the pan for 10 minutes before slicing and serving.

Lentil Loaf with Tomato Glaze offers a hearty and nutritious alternative to traditional meatloaf, featuring lentils as the main ingredient topped with a sweet and tangy tomato glaze. This low-cholesterol recipe is perfect for those seeking a satisfying and flavorful plant-based meal.

Nutritional Information: (per serving, approximate) Calories: 280, Protein: 12g, Carbohydrates: 40g, Fat: 8g, Fiber: 10g, Cholesterol: 0mg, Sodium: 400mg, Potassium: 500mg.

Baked Tofu with Teriyaki Glaze

 **4** servings  **15** minutes   **25** minutes

Ingredients:

- 1 block (14 ounces) extra-firm tofu, pressed and cut into 1-inch cubes
- 1/4 cup low-sodium soy sauce or tamari
- 2 tablespoons rice vinegar
- 1 tablespoon sesame oil
- 2 tablespoons maple syrup or honey
- 1 garlic clove, minced
- 1 teaspoon grated fresh ginger
- 1 tablespoon cornstarch
- 2 tablespoons water
- Sesame seeds for garnish
- Chopped green onions for garnish

Directions:

1. Preheat the oven to 400°F (200°C) and line a baking sheet with parchment paper.
2. Whisk soy sauce, rice vinegar, sesame oil, maple syrup, garlic, and ginger to make the marinade in a bowl.
3. Toss the tofu cubes in the marinade and sit for at least 10 minutes.
4. Place a single layer of marinated tofu on the prepared baking sheet. Bake for 25 minutes, flipping halfway through, until golden brown and crispy.
5. While tofu is baking, prepare the teriyaki glaze. Mix cornstarch and water in a small bowl. Pour the remaining marinade into a small saucepan, simmer, and add the cornstarch mixture. Cook, stirring constantly, until the sauce thickens into a glaze.
6. Toss the tofu in the teriyaki glaze once the tofu is baked.
7. Garnish with sesame seeds and chopped green onions.
8. Serve hot with your choice of sides, such as steamed rice and vegetables.

Baked Tofu with Teriyaki Glaze is a delicious and easy-to-make dish that coats firm tofu in a savory-sweet teriyaki glaze, resulting in a flavorful and satisfying meal. Ideal for a low-cholesterol diet, this recipe is perfect for those looking to enjoy a healthy, plant-based protein option.

Nutritional Information: (per serving, approximate) Calories: 160, Protein: 12g, Carbohydrates: 15g, Fat: 7g, Fiber: 2g, Cholesterol: 0mg, Sodium: 480mg, Potassium: 200mg.

Vegan Minestrone Soup

Ingredients:

 4 servings |  15 minutes | 30 minutes

- 1 tablespoon olive oil
- 1 onion, chopped
- 2 carrots, diced
- 2 celery stalks, diced
- 3 cloves garlic, minced
- 1 zucchini, diced
- 1 cup green beans, trimmed and cut into 1-inch pieces
- 1 can (14.5 ounces) diced tomatoes
- 4 cups low-sodium vegetable broth
- 1 can (15 ounces) cannellini beans, drained and rinsed
- 1 teaspoon dried oregano
- 1 teaspoon dried basil
- Salt and pepper to taste
- 1 cup whole wheat pasta (e.g., elbow macaroni or shells)
- 2 cups spinach leaves, roughly chopped

Directions:

1. In a large pot, heat olive oil over medium heat. Add onion, carrots, and celery. Cook until vegetables are softened, about 5 minutes.
2. Add garlic, zucchini, and green beans. Cook for another 3 minutes.
3. Stir in diced tomatoes, vegetable broth, cannellini beans, oregano, basil, salt, and pepper. Bring to a boil.
4. Add pasta and simmer until pasta is cooked, about 10 minutes.
5. Stir in spinach and cook until wilted, about 2 minutes.
6. Adjust seasoning if needed and serve hot.

This hearty and nutritious Vegan Minestrone Soup is perfect for a wholesome lunch or dinner. Packed with vegetables, beans, and whole wheat pasta, it's a comforting and satisfying meal that's low in cholesterol and high in fiber. It is ideal for anyone following a vegan or vegetarian diet.

Nutritional Information: (per serving, approximate) Calories: 250, Protein: 10g, Carbohydrates: 45g, Fat: 5g, Fiber: 10g, Cholesterol: 0mg, Sodium: 300mg, Potassium: 600mg.

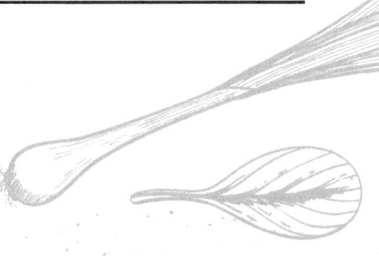

Stuffed Portobello Mushrooms with Spinach and Pecans

 4 servings |  15 minutes | 20 minutes

Ingredients:

- 4 large portobello mushrooms, stems, and gills removed
- 2 tablespoons olive oil
- 2 cloves garlic, minced
- 4 cups fresh spinach, chopped
- 1/2 cup pecans, chopped
- 1/4 cup grated Parmesan cheese (optional, can omit for vegan version)
- Salt and pepper to taste
- 1/4 teaspoon crushed red pepper flakes (optional)

Directions:

1. Preheat the oven to 375°F (190°C).
2. Brush the mushrooms with 1 tablespoon olive oil and place them on a baking sheet.
3. Heat the remaining olive oil over medium heat in a skillet. Add garlic and cook for 1 minute.
4. Add spinach to the skillet and cook until wilted, about 3 minutes. Stir in pecans, Parmesan cheese (if using), salt, pepper, and red pepper flakes.
5. Spoon the spinach and pecan mixture into the mushroom caps.
6. Bake in the preheated oven for 15-20 minutes, until the mushrooms are tender and the filling is heated.
7. Serve warm.

These Stuffed Portobello Mushrooms with Spinach and Pecans are a delicious and healthy option for a low-cholesterol diet. This dish is great as an appetizer, side, or even a light main course and can be easily adapted for vegan diets by omitting the Parmesan cheese.

Nutritional Information: (per serving, approximate) Calories: 200, Protein: 5g, Carbohydrates: 10g, Fat: 16g, Fiber: 3g, Cholesterol: 4mg, Sodium: 150mg, Potassium: 400mg.

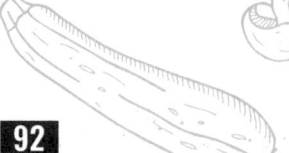

Mushroom and Barley Stew

Ingredients:

 4 servings  15 minutes  40 minutes

- 1 tablespoon olive oil
- 1 onion, chopped
- 2 cloves garlic, minced
- 2 cups mushrooms, sliced (e.g., cremini or button mushrooms)
- 1 cup pearl barley, rinsed
- 4 cups low-sodium vegetable broth
- 2 carrots, peeled and diced
- 2 celery stalks, diced
- 1 teaspoon dried thyme
- Salt and pepper to taste
- 2 tablespoons fresh parsley, chopped

Directions:

1. Heat olive oil in a large pot over medium heat. Add onion and garlic, and sauté until softened, about 5 minutes.
2. Add mushrooms and cook for another 5 minutes until they start to release their juices.
3. Stir in barley, vegetable broth, carrots, celery, thyme, salt, and pepper.
4. Bring to a boil, then reduce heat, cover, and simmer for 30-35 minutes, until barley is tender and the stew has thickened.
5. Adjust seasoning as needed and stir in fresh parsley before serving.
6. Serve hot as a hearty and warm meal.

This Mushroom and Barley Stew is a comforting and nutritious choice for anyone following a low-cholesterol diet. The stew is perfect for a cozy dinner and offers a hearty, satisfying meal with plenty of fiber and flavor.

Nutritional Information: (per serving, approximate) Calories:220, Protein: 8g, Carbohydrates: 44g, Fat: 4g, Fiber: 9g, Cholesterol: 0mg, Sodium: 200mg, Potassium: 450mg.

Vegan Falafel Bowl
with Hummus and Tahini

Ingredients:

- 1 cup dried chickpeas, soaked overnight and drained
- 1 small onion, chopped
- 2 cloves garlic, minced
- 1/4 cup fresh parsley, chopped
- 1 teaspoon ground cumin (optional)
- 1 teaspoon ground coriander (optional)
- Salt and pepper to taste
- 2 tablespoons all-purpose flour
- 4 cups mixed salad greens
- 1 cup cherry tomatoes, halved
- 1 cucumber, sliced
- 1/2 cup hummus
- 1/4 cup tahini
- 2 tablespoons lemon juice
- 1 tablespoon olive oil

 4 servings |  20 minutes | 30 minutes

Directions:

1. Preheat the oven to 375°F (190°C). Line a baking sheet with parchment paper.
2. Combine soaked chickpeas, onion, garlic, parsley, cumin, coriander, salt, pepper, and flour in a food processor. Pulse until well combined but still slightly coarse.
3. Place the mixture into small balls or patties on the prepared baking sheet.
4. Bake for 25-30 minutes, flipping halfway, until golden and crispy.
5. Prepare the bowls by dividing the mixed salad greens, cherry tomatoes, and cucumber among four bowls.
6. Top each bowl with baked falafel, a dollop of hummus, and a drizzle of tahini mixed with lemon juice and olive oil.
7. Serve immediately as a nutritious and flavorful vegan meal.

Description: The Vegan Falafel Bowl with Hummus and Tahini is a delightful, nutrient-packed meal perfect for anyone on a low-cholesterol diet. It's ideal for a satisfying lunch or dinner and will surely please vegans and non-vegans alike.

Nutritional Information: (per serving, approximate) Calories:320, Protein: 14g, Carbohydrates: 45g, Fat:12g, Fiber: 10g, Cholesterol: 0mg, Sodium: 310mg, Potassium: 600mg.

Creamy Pumpkin and Lentil Soup

Ingredients:

 4 servings | 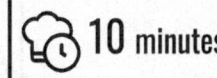 10 minutes | 30 minutes

- 1 tablespoon olive oil
- 1 onion, finely chopped
- 2 cloves garlic, minced
- 1 teaspoon ground cumin (optional)
- 1 teaspoon ground coriander (optional)
- 1/2 teaspoon ground ginger (optional)
- 1 cup red lentils, rinsed and drained
- 4 cups low-sodium vegetable broth
- 1 can (15 oz) pumpkin puree
- Salt and pepper to taste
- 1/2 cup light coconut milk
- Fresh cilantro, chopped, for garnish

Directions:

1. Heat olive oil in a large pot over medium heat. Add onion and garlic, sautéing until softened, about 5 minutes.
2. Stir in cumin, coriander, and ginger, cooking for another minute until fragrant.
3. Add red lentils and vegetable broth. Bring to a boil, then reduce heat and simmer for 20 minutes until lentils are tender.
4. Stir in pumpkin puree and continue to simmer for an additional 5 minutes.
5. Use an immersion blender to puree the soup until smooth. Season with salt and pepper to taste.
6. Stir in coconut milk and heat through.
7. Serve hot, garnished with fresh cilantro.

Creamy Pumpkin and Lentil Soup is a heartwarming and nutritious dish perfect for a cozy meal. It's a fantastic combination of savory spices, tender lentils, and smooth pumpkin puree, all blended into a creamy delight with a hint of coconut milk.

Nutritional Information: (per serving, approximate) Calories: 280, Protein: 14g, Carbohydrates: 45g, Fat: 6g, Fiber: 18g, Cholesterol: 0mg, Sodium: 200mg, Potassium: 730mg.

Vegan Pad Thai with Tofu

Ingredients:

- 8 oz rice noodles
- 1 block of firm tofu, drained and cubed
- 2 tablespoons vegetable oil
- 1 red bell pepper, thinly sliced
- 1 carrot, julienned
- 2 green onions, chopped
- 2 cloves garlic, minced
- 1/4 cup low-sodium soy sauce
- 2 tablespoons brown sugar
- 2 tablespoons tamarind paste
- 1 tablespoon lime juice
- 1/4 cup chopped peanuts
- 1/4 cup fresh cilantro, chopped
- Lime wedges for serving

 4 servings  10 minutes | 30 minutes

Directions:

1. Prepare rice noodles according to package instructions. Drain and set aside.
2. Heat oil in a large skillet over medium heat. Add tofu and cook until golden brown, about 5 minutes. Remove tofu from the skillet and set aside.
3. In the same skillet, add red bell pepper, carrot, green onions, and garlic. Stir-fry for about 3 minutes.
4. Whisk soy sauce, brown sugar, tamarind paste, and lime juice in a small bowl.
5. Add cooked noodles and tofu back to the skillet. Pour the sauce over and toss to combine.
6. Cook for another 2 minutes until everything is heated and well-coated with the sauce.
7. Serve garnished with chopped peanuts, cilantro, and lime wedges on the side.

Vegan Pad Thai with Tofu is a delightful twist on the classic Thai dish. This version is loaded with colorful vegetables, chewy rice noodles, and crispy tofu, all tossed in a tangy and slightly sweet sauce. It perfectly balances flavors and textures, offering a satisfying and nutritious meal. The dish is high in protein and fiber, making it an ideal choice for those on a low-cholesterol diet.

Nutritional Information: (per serving, approximate) Calories:350, Protein: 15g, Carbohydrates: 56g, Fat: 9g, Fiber: 3g, Cholesterol: 0mg, Sodium: 530mg, Potassium: 250mg.

Ratatouille with Crispy Polenta

Ingredients:

- 1 eggplant, diced
- 2 zucchinis, diced
- 1 red bell pepper, diced
- 1 yellow bell pepper, diced
- 1 onion, chopped
- 3 cloves garlic, minced
- 1 can (28 oz) diced tomatoes
- 2 tablespoons olive oil
- 1 teaspoon dried thyme
- 1 teaspoon dried basil
- Salt and pepper to taste
- 1 package pre-cooked polenta, sliced into rounds
- Cooking spray

 4 servings    20 minutes    40 minutes

Directions:

1. Preheat oven to 375°F (190°C).
2. In a large skillet, heat olive oil over medium heat. Add onion and garlic, and cook until softened.
3. Add eggplant, zucchini, and bell peppers. Cook for about 5 minutes.
4. Add diced tomatoes, thyme, basil, salt, and pepper. Simmer for 20 minutes.
5. While ratatouille is cooking, spray a baking sheet with cooking spray. Place polenta rounds on the sheet and spray the tops with cooking spray.
6. Bake polenta in the oven for 15-20 minutes or until crispy.
7. Serve ratatouille hot over crispy polenta rounds.

Ratatouille with Crispy Polenta is a delightful vegetarian dish that combines the rich flavors of traditional French ratatouille with the satisfying crunch of baked polenta. This low-cholesterol recipe is ideal for a hearty lunch or dinner and can be served as a main or a side dish. It's a flavorful, colorful, and healthy choice for anyone following a low-cholesterol diet.

Nutritional Information: (per serving, approximate) Calories: 280, Protein: 6g, Carbohydrates: 45g, Fat: 9g, Fiber: 8g, Cholesterol: 0mg, Sodium: 480mg, Potassium: 750mg.

Vegan Shepherd's Pie

Ingredients:

 4 servings 20 minutes 40 minutes

- 2 large sweet potatoes, peeled and cubed
- 1 tablespoon olive oil
- 1 onion, chopped
- 2 cloves garlic, minced
- 1 carrot, diced
- 1 cup frozen peas
- 1 cup cooked lentils
- 1 tablespoon tomato paste
- 1 teaspoon dried thyme (optional)
- 1/2 teaspoon paprika
- Salt and pepper to taste
- 1/4 cup unsweetened almond milk
- 2 tablespoons vegan butter

Directions:

1. Preheat oven to 375°F (190°C).
2. In a large skillet, heat olive oil over medium heat. Add onion and garlic, and cook until softened.
3. Add eggplant, zucchini, and bell peppers. Cook for about 5 minutes.
4. Add diced tomatoes, thyme, basil, salt, and pepper. Simmer for 20 minutes.
5. While ratatouille is cooking, spray a baking sheet with cooking spray. Place polenta rounds on the sheet and spray the tops with cooking spray.
6. Bake polenta in the oven for 15-20 minutes or until crispy.
7. Serve ratatouille hot over crispy polenta rounds.

This Vegan Shepherd's Pie is a delicious and comforting dish that replaces traditional meat with a hearty mixture of lentils and vegetables, topped with a creamy sweet potato mash. It's a satisfying and nourishing meal perfect for a cozy dinner.

Nutritional Information: (per serving, approximate) Calories: 290, Protein: 10g, Carbohydrates: 55g, Fat: 5g, Fiber: 11g, Cholesterol: 0mg, Sodium: 160mg, Potassium: 790mg.

Roasted Vegetable Paella

Ingredients:

 4 servings  20 minutes 40 minutes

- 1 red bell pepper, sliced
- 1 yellow bell pepper, sliced
- 1 zucchini, sliced
- 1 red onion, chopped
- 2 tomatoes, diced
- 2 cloves garlic, minced
- 1 cup short-grain brown rice
- 1 teaspoon smoked paprika
- 1/2 teaspoon saffron threads
- 2 1/2 cups low-sodium vegetable broth
- 1 cup frozen peas
- Salt and pepper to taste
- 2 tablespoons olive oil
- Fresh parsley, chopped for garnish
- Lemon wedges for serving

Directions:

1. Toss chopped bell peppers, zucchini, and onion with 1 tablespoon oil, salt, and pepper. Preheat the oven to 400°F (200°C) and roast the vegetables on a baking sheet for 20 minutes until tender and browned.
2. Heat remaining olive oil over medium heat in a large skillet. Add minced garlic and cook until fragrant, about 1 minute.
3. Add rice, smoked paprika and saffron threads. Cook for 2 minutes.
4. Add diced tomatoes and vegetable broth to the pan. Bring to a boil, cover and simmer over low heat for 20 minutes until the rice is almost tender.
5. Fried vegetables can be cut into smaller pieces.
6. Stir fried vegetables and frozen peas into a pan with rice. Cook for another 5 minutes until the rice is done.
7. Season the paella with salt and pepper to taste. Garnish with chopped parsley and serve hot with lemon wedges.

This Vegan Shepherd's Pie is a delicious and comforting dish that replaces traditional meat with a hearty mixture of lentils and vegetables, topped with a creamy sweet potato mash. It's a satisfying and nourishing meal perfect for a cozy dinner.

Nutritional Information: (per serving, approximate) Calories: 290, Protein: 10g, Carbohydrates: 55g, Fat: 5g, Fiber: 11g, Cholesterol: 0mg, Sodium: 160mg, Potassium: 790mg.

Red Lentil Dal with Spinach

Ingredients:

- 1 cup red lentils, rinsed
- 1 onion, finely chopped
- 2 cloves garlic, minced
- 1 tablespoon ginger, grated
- 1 teaspoon ground turmeric
- 1 teaspoon ground cumin (optional)
- 1/2 teaspoon ground coriander (optional)
- 1/4 teaspoon cayenne pepper (optional)
- 4 cups vegetable broth
- 3 cups fresh spinach, chopped
- 1 tablespoon lemon juice
- Salt to taste
- 2 tablespoons olive oil

 4 servings    10 minutes   25 minutes

Directions:

1. Heat olive oil in a large pot over medium heat. Add onion, garlic, and ginger. Cook until onion is translucent.
2. Stir in turmeric, cumin, coriander, and cayenne pepper. Cook for 1 minute.
3. Add red lentils and vegetable broth. Bring to a boil, then reduce heat and simmer for 20 minutes until lentils are soft.
4. Stir in chopped spinach and cook until wilted about 3 minutes.
5. Add lemon juice and salt to taste. Adjust seasoning as needed.
6. Serve hot, optionally garnished with fresh herbs or a dollop of yogurt.

This Red Lentil Dal with Spinach is a nutritious and flavorful vegetarian dish, perfect for a comforting meal.

Nutritional Information: (per serving, approximate) Calories: 240, Protein: 15g, Carbohydrates: 35g, Fat: 5g, Fiber: 15g, Cholesterol: 0mg, Sodium: 480mg, Potassium: 680mg.

Vegan Mushroom Risotto

Ingredients:

- 2 tablespoons olive oil
- 1 small onion, finely chopped
- 2 cloves garlic, minced
- 1 cup Arborio rice
- 1/2 cup dry white wine (optional)
- 4 cups low-sodium vegetable broth, heated
- 2 cups sliced mushrooms (button or cremini)
- 1 teaspoon dried thyme
- Salt and pepper to taste
- 1/4 cup nutritional yeast (or more to taste)
- Fresh parsley, chopped for garnish

 4 servings    10 minutes   30 minutes

Directions:

1. Heat olive oil in a large skillet over medium heat. Add onions and garlic, sautéing until softened.
2. Stir in Arborio rice, toasting for 2 minutes.
3. Pour in white wine (if using) and cook until evaporated.
4. Add a ladleful of hot vegetable broth to the rice, stirring constantly. Once absorbed, add another ladleful, continuing until all broth is used and the rice is creamy and al dente.
5. In a separate pan, sauté mushrooms with thyme, salt, and pepper until cooked.
6. Mix mushrooms into the risotto, then stir in nutritional yeast. Adjust seasoning.
7. Serve hot, garnished with fresh parsley.

This Vegan Mushroom Risotto is a comforting and hearty dish perfect for a low-cholesterol diet. It's a versatile and nourishing meal that's sure to please vegans and non-vegans alike.

Nutritional Information: (per serving, approximate) Calories:310, Protein: 9g, Carbohydrates: 53g, Fat: 7g, Fiber: 4g, Cholesterol: 0mg, Sodium: 200mg, Potassium: 350mg.

Summer Berry Splash

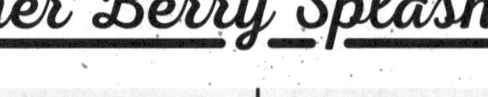

Ingredients:

- 1 cup fresh strawberries, halved
- 1 cup fresh blueberries
- 1 cup fresh raspberries
- 1/2 lemon, juiced
- 2 tablespoons honey (adjust to taste)
- 4 cups sparkling water, chilled
- Ice cubes (optional)
- Fresh mint leaves for garnish

This recipe is a perfect low-cholesterol, refreshing drink for the summer, providing a delicious way to enjoy the bounty of fresh berries while keeping your health in check.

 4 servings  10 minutes  0 minutes

Directions:

1. Combine strawberries, blueberries, raspberries, lemon juice, and honey in a blender. Blend until smooth.
2. Strain the berry mixture through a fine mesh sieve into a large pitcher, pressing on the solids to extract as much liquid as possible. Discard solids.
3. Add sparkling water to the pitcher with the berry juice and stir gently to combine.
4. Fill glasses with ice cubes (if using) and pour the Summer Berry Splash over the ice.
5. Garnish with fresh mint leaves.
6. Serve immediately and enjoy the refreshing taste.

Nutritional Information: (per serving, approximate) Calories: 80, Protein: 1 g, Carbohydrates: 21 g, Fat: 0.5 g, Fiber: 4 g, Cholesterol: 0 mg, Sodium: 10 mg, Potassium: 200 mg.

Virgin Strawberry Basil Mojito

Ingredients:

- 1 cup fresh strawberries, quartered
- 1/4 cup fresh basil leaves, plus more for garnish
- 2 tablespoons lime juice, freshly squeezed
- 1-2 tablespoons agave syrup or honey (adjust to taste)
- 4 cups sparkling water or club soda, chilled
- Ice cubes
- Lime slices and whole strawberries for garnish

Enjoy this refreshing and health-conscious Virgin Strawberry Basil Mojito, perfect for any occasion that calls for a burst of flavor without guilt!

 4 servings  15 minutes 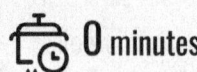 0 minutes

Directions:

1. In a large pitcher, muddle the strawberries and basil leaves with the lime juice and agave syrup (or honey) until the strawberries are slightly mashed and the basil is fragrant.
2. Add the sparkling water or club soda to the pitcher and stir gently to combine.
3. Fill glasses with ice cubes and evenly distribute the mojito mixture among the glasses.
4. Garnish each glass with lime slices, whole strawberries, and a sprig of basil.
5. Serve immediately, stirring each glass gently before drinking to mix the flavors.

Nutritional Information: (per serving, approximate) Calories: 50, Protein: 0.5 g, Carbohydrates: 13 g, Fat: 0 g, Fiber: 2 g, Cholesterol: 0 mg, Sodium: 5 mg, Potassium: 145 mg

Mango Passion Fruit Fizz

Ingredients:

- 1 ripe mango, peeled and cubed
- Pulp of 2 passion fruits
- 2 tablespoons lime juice
- 2-3 tablespoons honey or agave syrup (adjust to taste)
- 4 cups sparkling water, chilled
- Ice cubes
- Lime slices or mint leaves for garnish

This Mango Passion Fruit Fizz is a delightful, low-cholesterol refreshment perfect for enjoying a warm day or serving at a summer party. Bursting with tropical flavors, it's both delicious and healthy.

 4 servings |  10 minutes |  0 minutes

Directions:

1. Combine mango cubes, passion fruit pulp, lime juice, and honey or agave syrup in a blender. Blend until smooth.
2. Strain the mixture through a fine mesh sieve into a pitcher, discarding any solids to ensure a smooth drink.
3. Add sparkling water to the pitcher and stir gently to mix.
4. Fill glasses with ice cubes and pour the Mango Passion Fruit Fizz over the ice.
5. Garnish each glass with a slice of lime or a mint leaf for a refreshing touch.
6. Serve immediately to enjoy a tropical, fizzy, and refreshing drink.

Nutritional Information: (per serving, approximate) Calories: 80, Protein: 1 g, Carbohydrates: 20 g, Fat: 0.2 g, Fiber: 2 g, Cholesterol: 0 mg, Sodium: 10 mg, Potassium: 180 mg

Summer Peach Sparkle

Ingredients:

- 2 ripe peaches, pitted and sliced
- 1 tablespoon honey or agave syrup (adjust to taste)
- 4 cups sparkling water, chilled
- Juice of 1 lemon
- Ice cubes
- Peach slices and fresh raspberries for garnish

Enjoy this low-cholesterol, deliciously refreshing Summer Peach Sparkle, perfect for any summer gathering or a relaxing day in the sun. Bursting with the sweet taste of fresh peaches and the tanginess of lemon, it's a delightful drink that's both healthy and hydrating.

 4 servings |  10 minutes |  0 minutes

Directions:

1. Combine the peach slices, lemon juice, and honey or agave syrup in a blender. Blend until smooth.
2. Strain the peach mixture through a fine mesh sieve into a pitcher, discarding the solids to ensure a smooth texture.
3. Add the sparkling water to the pitcher and stir gently to mix well.
4. Fill glasses with ice cubes and pour the Summer Peach Sparkle over the ice.
5. Garnish each glass with additional peach slices and fresh raspberries for a touch of elegance and extra flavor.
6. Serve immediately, offering a refreshingly light and bubbly mocktail that captures the essence of summer.

Nutritional Information: (per serving, approximate) Calories: 60, Protein: 1 g, Carbohydrates: 15 g, Fat: 0.2 g, Fiber: 2 g, Cholesterol: 0 mg, Sodium: 10 mg, Potassium: 150 mg

Watermelon Lime Quencher

Ingredients:

 4 servings  15 minutes 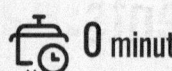 0 minutes

- 4 cups cubed seedless watermelon
- Juice of 2 limes
- 2-3 tablespoons honey or agave syrup (optional, adjust to taste)
- 4 cups chilled sparkling water
- Ice cubes
- Lime slices and watermelon wedges for garnish

This Watermelon Lime Quencher is a low-cholesterol, delightfully refreshing mocktail perfect for summer festivities or simply enjoying a relaxing moment. Bursting with the fresh flavors of watermelon and lime, it's sure to be a hit with everyone.

Directions:

1. Place the watermelon cubes in a blender and blend until smooth.
2. Strain the watermelon puree through a fine mesh sieve into a pitcher, pressing on the solids to extract as much juice as possible. Discard the solids.
3. Stir in the lime juice and honey or agave syrup into the watermelon juice until well combined.
4. Just before serving, add the sparkling water to the pitcher and gently stir to mix.
5. Fill glasses with ice cubes, pour the Watermelon Lime Quencher over the ice, and garnish each glass with a lime slice and a watermelon wedge.
6. Serve immediately for a refreshing and hydrating drink perfect for cooling down on a hot day.

Nutritional Information: (per serving, approximate) Calories: 60, Protein: 1 g, Carbohydrates: 15 g, Fat: 0.2 g, Fiber: 0.6 g, Cholesterol: 0 mg, Sodium: 10 mg, Potassium: 170 mg.

Blueberry Bliss Soda

Ingredients:

 4 servings  10 minutes 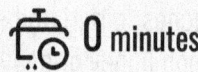 0 minutes

- 1 cup fresh blueberries, plus extra for garnish
- 1/4 cup lemon juice, freshly squeezed
- 3 tablespoons honey or agave syrup (adjust to taste)
- 4 cups sparkling water, chilled
- Ice cubes
- Fresh mint leaves for garnish

Enjoy this low-cholesterol, vibrant Blueberry Bliss Soda, a refreshing and healthful drink that combines the sweet and tart flavors of blueberries and lemon with the fizz of sparkling water.

Directions:

1. Combine the fresh blueberries, lemon juice, and honey or agave syrup in a blender. Blend until smooth.
2. Strain the mixture through a fine mesh sieve into a pitcher to remove the solids, ensuring a smooth liquid.
3. Add the sparkling water to the pitcher and stir gently to combine.
4. Fill glasses with ice cubes and pour the Blueberry Bliss Soda over the ice.
5. Garnish each glass with a few fresh blueberries and a sprig of mint for a refreshing touch.
6. Serve immediately, offering a delightful and effervescent mocktail perfect for any occasion.

Nutritional Information: (per serving, approximate) Calories: 60, Protein: 0.5 g, Carbohydrates: 16 g, Fat: 0.2 g, Fiber: 2 g, Cholesterol: 0 mg, Sodium: 10 mg, Potassium: 55 mg

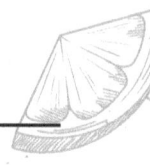

Carrot Orange Spice Mocktail

Ingredients:

- 2 cups fresh carrot juice (about 6-8 large carrots, juiced)
- 2 cups fresh orange juice (about 4-6 oranges, juiced)
- 1/2 teaspoon ground cinnamon
- 1/4 teaspoon ground nutmeg
- 1 teaspoon vanilla extract
- Ice cubes
- Orange slices and cinnamon sticks for garnish

This revised Carrot Orange Spice Mocktail, cinnamon, and nutmeg bring warmth and depth to the drink, making it an ideal choice for those looking for a nutritious, low-cholesterol beverage with a comforting spice blend.

 4 servings  15 minutes  0 minutes

Directions:

1. Combine the fresh carrot juice, fresh orange juice, ground cinnamon, ground nutmeg, and vanilla extract in a large pitcher. Stir well to ensure all the spices are fully integrated into the juices.
2. Refrigerate the mixture for at least 1 hour to allow the flavors to meld together and the drink to chill thoroughly.
3. To serve, fill glasses with ice cubes and pour the chilled Carrot Orange Spice Mocktail over the ice.
4. Garnish each glass with an orange slice and a cinnamon stick for a festive and aromatic touch.
5. Serve immediately, offering your guests a flavorful and refreshing mocktail that's perfect for any season.

Nutritional Information: (per serving, approximate) Calories: 125, Protein: 2 g, Carbohydrates: 29 g, Fat: 0.5 g, Fiber: 1 g, Cholesterol: 0 mg, Sodium: 70 mg, Potassium: 700 mg

Sparkling Cranberry Kombucha

Ingredients:

- 2 cups cranberry juice (unsweetened)
- 2 cups kombucha (plain or ginger-flavored)
- Ice cubes
- Fresh cranberries for garnish
- Rosemary sprigs for garnish

This Sparkling Cranberry Kombucha mocktail combines the tangy taste of cranberry with the gut-friendly probiotics of kombucha, making it a delightful low-cholesterol beverage and a healthy choice for your gut.

 4 servings  5 minutes 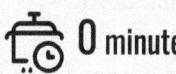 0 minutes

Directions:

1. In a pitcher, combine the cranberry juice and kombucha. Stir gently to mix well.
2. Place the pitcher in the refrigerator to chill until ready to serve, or proceed to the next step for immediate serving.
3. Fill glasses with ice cubes to keep the mocktail cold.
4. Pour the Sparkling Cranberry Kombucha mixture over the ice in each glass.
5. Garnish each glass with a few fresh cranberries and a sprig of rosemary for a festive touch.
6. Serve immediately, offering a tangy and refreshing mocktail with the added health benefits of kombucha.

Nutritional Information: (per serving, approximate) Calories: 80, Protein: 0 g, Carbohydrates: 20 g, Fat: 0 g, Fiber: 0 g, Cholesterol: 0 mg, Sodium: 10 mg, Potassium: 150 mg

Tropical Turmeric Cooler

Ingredients:

- 2 cups pineapple juice
- 1 cup coconut water
- 1/2 teaspoon ground turmeric
- Juice of 1 lime
- 1 tablespoon honey or agave syrup (optional, adjust to taste)
- Ice cubes
- Pineapple slices and lime wedges for garnish

This Tropical Turmeric Cooler is a vibrant, low-cholesterol mocktail that combines the sweet and tangy flavors of pineapple and lime with the healthful benefits of turmeric and coconut water. It's a perfect refreshing drink to enjoy on a hot day or as a nutritious start to your morning.

  **4 servings** | **10 minutes** |  **0 minutes**

Directions:

1. Combine the pineapple juice, coconut water, ground turmeric, lime juice, and honey or agave syrup in a large pitcher. Stir well until all the ingredients are fully integrated and the honey is dissolved.
2. Taste the mixture and adjust the sweetness if necessary by adding a bit more honey or agave syrup.
3. Refrigerate the mixture for at least 30 minutes to allow the flavors to meld together and the drink to chill.
4. When ready to serve, fill glasses with ice cubes to keep the mocktail cold.
5. Pour the Tropical Turmeric Cooler over the ice in each glass.
6. Garnish each glass with a pineapple slice and a lime wedge for a tropical presentation.
7. Serve immediately, offering a refreshingly healthy and invigorating mocktail perfect for any time of day.

Nutritional Information: (per serving, approximate) Calories: 80, Protein: 0.5 g, Carbohydrates: 19 g, Fat: 0.2 g, Fiber: 0.5 g, Cholesterol: 0 mg, Sodium: 30 mg, Potassium: 200 mg

Berry Hibiscus Delight

Ingredients:

- 4 hibiscus tea bags
- 2 cups boiling water
- 1 cup mixed berries (such as strawberries, raspberries, and blueberries), fresh or frozen
- 2 tablespoons honey or agave syrup
- 2 cups cold water
- Ice cubes
- Additional berries and lemon slices for garnish

This Berry Hibiscus Delight mocktail combines the tangy flavor of hibiscus tea with the natural sweetness of mixed berries, creating a delicious and healthful beverage that's low in cholesterol and perfect for sipping on a warm day.

  **4 servings** | **10 minutes + CHILLING TIME** |  **0 minutes**

Directions:

1. Steep the hibiscus tea bags in 2 cups of boiling water for 5 minutes. Remove the tea bags after steeping.
2. While the tea is warm, stir in the honey or agave syrup until dissolved.
3. Blend the 1 cup of mixed berries until smooth in a blender.
4. Strain the berry puree through a fine mesh sieve into the tea mixture, pressing on the solids to extract as much liquid as possible. Discard the solids.
5. Add 2 cups of cold water to the tea and berry mixture. Stir well and refrigerate until chilled.
6. To serve, fill glasses with ice cubes, pour the Berry Hibiscus Delight over the ice, and garnish each glass with additional berries and a slice of lemon.
7. Serve chilled, offering a refreshingly tart and fruity mocktail perfect for any occasion.

Nutritional Information: (per serving, approximate) Calories: 50, Protein: 0.5 g, Carbohydrates: 13 g, Fat: 0 g, Fiber: 1 g, Cholesterol: 0 mg, Sodium: 10 mg, Potassium: 50 mg

Blueberry Lavender Smash

Ingredients:

- 1 cup fresh blueberries, plus extra for garnish
- 2 teaspoons dried lavender flowers
- 4 tablespoons honey or agave syrup (adjust to taste)
- Juice of 2 lemons
- 4 cups sparkling water, chilled
- Ice cubes
- Lavender sprigs for garnish

The Blueberry Lavender Smash is a low-cholesterol, beautifully crafted mocktail that combines the sweetness of blueberries with the soothing aroma of lavender, topped with the fizz of sparkling water, for a refreshing and elegant drink suitable for any occasion.

 4 servings    15 minutes    0 minutes

Directions:

1. In a small bowl, muddle the blueberries with the dried lavender flowers and honey or agave syrup until the blueberries are smashed and the mixture is fragrant.
2. Divide the blueberry-lavender mixture evenly among four glasses.
3. Squeeze the juice of half a lemon into each glass.
4. Fill each glass with ice cubes, then top off with sparkling water.
5. Use a spoon to gently stir the mixture in each glass, combining the flavors.
6. Garnish each glass with a few fresh blueberries and a sprig of lavender.
7. Serve immediately, offering a refreshing, aromatic mocktail with a delightful blend of blueberry and lavender flavors.

Nutritional Information: (per serving, approximate) Calories: 80, Protein: 0.5 g, Carbohydrates: 20 g, Fat: 0.2 g, Fiber: 2 g, Cholesterol: 0 mg, Sodium: 10 mg, Potassium: 55 mg

---

Cucumber Basil Sparkle

Ingredients:

- 1 large cucumber, sliced thinly
- 1/4 cup fresh basil leaves, plus extra for garnish
- 2 tablespoons lime juice, freshly squeezed
- 3 tablespoons honey or agave syrup (adjust to taste)
- 4 cups sparkling water, chilled
- Ice cubes
- Lime slices for garnish

This Cucumber Basil Sparkle mocktail is a low-cholesterol, invigorating drink that combines the crisp taste of cucumber with the aromatic freshness of basil and the tanginess of lime, topped with the fizz of sparkling water for a delightful beverage experience.

 4 servings    10 minutes   0 minutes

Directions:

1. In a pitcher, muddle the cucumber slices, and basil leaves with the lime juice and honey or agave syrup until the cucumber is slightly crushed and the basil is fragrant.
2. Add the sparkling water to the pitcher and stir gently to combine all the ingredients.
3. Let the mixture chill in the refrigerator for about 30 minutes to enhance the flavors.
4. Fill glasses with ice cubes and strain the Cucumber Basil Sparkle into the glasses, discarding the solids.
5. Garnish each glass with a slice of lime and a sprig of basil.
6. Serve immediately, offering a refreshingly light and hydrating mocktail perfect for any time of day.

Nutritional Information: (per serving, approximate) Calories: 50, Protein: 0.5 g, Carbohydrates: 13 g, Fat: 0.1 g, Fiber: 0.5 g, Cholesterol: 0 mg, Sodium: 15 mg, Potassium: 75 mg

Avocado Berry Bliss

Ingredients:

- 1 ripe avocado, peeled and pitted
- 1 cup fresh or frozen mixed berries (such as strawberries, blueberries, raspberries)
- 1 banana, sliced
- 2 cups almond milk, unsweetened
- 1 tablespoon honey or agave syrup (optional, adjust to taste)
- Ice cubes (optional if using fresh berries)

This Avocado Berry Bliss smoothie combines the creamy texture of avocado with the sweet and tangy flavors of mixed berries, balanced with the subtle sweetness of banana and almond milk, making it a deliciously healthy, low-cholesterol option for any time of the day.

 4 servings  5 minutes  0 minutes

Directions:

1. Combine the avocado, mixed berries, banana, almond milk, and honey or agave syrup in a blender.
2. Blend on high speed until the mixture is smooth and creamy. Add more almond milk to reach your desired consistency if the smoothie is too thick.
3. If you're using fresh berries and prefer a colder smoothie, add a handful of ice cubes to the blender and blend until smooth.
4. Taste the smoothie and adjust the sweetness if necessary by adding a bit more honey or agave syrup.
5. Pour the smoothie into glasses and serve immediately.
6. Enjoy the creamy texture and rich flavors of the Avocado Berry Bliss, a perfect start to your day or a refreshing snack.

Nutritional Information: (per serving, approximate) Calories: 180, Protein: 3 g, Carbohydrates: 24 g, Fat: 9 g, Fiber: 7 g, Cholesterol: 0 mg, Sodium: 80 mg, Potassium: 450 mg

Golden Milk Mango Smoothie

Ingredients:

- 2 cups frozen mango chunks
- 1 banana, sliced
- 2 cups almond milk, unsweetened
- 1/2 teaspoon ground turmeric
- 1/4 teaspoon ground cinnamon
- 1/4 teaspoon ground ginger
- 1 tablespoon honey or agave syrup (optional, adjust to taste)
- A pinch of black pepper (to enhance turmeric absorption)

This Golden Milk Mango Smoothie blends the tropical sweetness of mango with the healthful spices of golden milk for a nourishing, low-cholesterol drink that's perfect for starting your day or as a refreshing snack.

 4 servings 5 minutes 0 minutes

Directions:

1. In a blender, combine the frozen mango chunks, banana, almond milk, ground turmeric, ground cinnamon, ground ginger, honey (or agave syrup), and a pinch of black pepper.
2. Blend on high speed until the mixture is smooth and creamy. Add more almond milk to reach your desired consistency if the smoothie is too thick.
3. Taste the smoothie and adjust the sweetness if necessary by adding a bit more honey or agave syrup.
4. Pour the smoothie into glasses and serve immediately.
5. Enjoy the unique combination of sweet mango and banana with the warming turmeric, cinnamon, and ginger spices, creating a deliciously healthy and invigorating Golden Milk Mango Smoothie.

Nutritional Information: (per serving, approximate) Calories: 150, Protein: 2 g, Carbohydrates: 33 g, Fat: 2 g, Fiber: 3 g, Cholesterol: 0 mg, Sodium: 80 mg, Potassium: 400 mg

Spinach Pear Cleanse

Ingredients:

- 2 ripe pears, cored and chopped
- 2 cups fresh spinach leaves
- 1 banana, sliced
- 2 tablespoons chia seeds
- 2 cups almond milk, unsweetened
- Ice cubes (optional)

This Spinach Pear Cleanse smoothie combines the natural sweetness of ripe pears with the nutrient-dense qualities of spinach and the added benefits of chia seeds for a potent, low-cholesterol drink that supports overall health and wellness.

 4 servings 5 minutes 0 minutes

Directions:

1. Combine the chopped pears, fresh spinach leaves, sliced banana, chia seeds, and almond milk in a blender.
2. Blend at high speed until the mixture is smooth. If you prefer a colder smoothie, add a handful of ice cubes to the blender and blend until smooth.
3. Taste the smoothie and adjust the consistency if necessary by adding more almond milk.
4. Once the smoothie reaches your desired consistency, pour it into glasses.
5. Serve immediately, offering a nutrient-rich and detoxifying Spinach Pear Cleanse smoothie perfect for a refreshing start to your day or a healthy midday snack.

Nutritional Information: (per serving, approximate) Calories: 150, Protein: 3 g, Carbohydrates: 27 g, Fat: 4 g, Fiber: 6 g, Cholesterol: 0 mg, Sodium: 90 mg, Potassium: 400 mg

---

Chocolate Almond Butter Smoothie

Ingredients:

- 2 bananas, sliced and frozen
- 2 tablespoons almond butter
- 2 tablespoons cocoa powder, unsweetened
- 2 cups almond milk, unsweetened
- 1 tablespoon honey or agave syrup (optional, adjust to taste)
- Ice cubes (optional for a thicker smoothie)

This Chocolate Almond Butter Smoothie combines the creamy texture of almond butter with the rich, indulgent flavor of cocoa powder, balanced with the natural sweetness of bananas and almond milk for a deliciously healthy, low-cholesterol treat.

 4 servings 5 minutes 0 minutes

Directions:

1. Combine the frozen banana slices, almond butter, cocoa powder, almond milk, and honey or agave syrup in a blender.
2. Blend on high speed until the mixture is smooth and creamy. If the smoothie is too thick or too thin for your liking, adjust the consistency by adding more almond milk or ice cubes and blending again.
3. Taste the smoothie and adjust the sweetness if necessary by adding a bit more honey or agave syrup.
4. Once the smoothie reaches your desired consistency and taste, pour it into glasses.
5. Serve immediately. Offering a rich and indulgent Chocolate Almond Butter Smoothie that's perfect for satisfying your sweet tooth while keeping your cholesterol in check.

Nutritional Information: (per serving, approximate) Calories: 180, Protein: 4 g, Carbohydrates: 27 g, Fat: 7 g, Fiber: 4 g, Cholesterol: 0 mg, Sodium: 90 mg, Potassium: 400 mg

Cherry Vanilla Antioxidant Smoothie

Ingredients:

- 2 cups frozen cherries, pitted
- 1 banana, sliced
- 1 teaspoon vanilla extract
- 2 cups almond milk, unsweetened
- 2 tablespoons honey or agave syrup (optional, adjust to taste)
- Ice cubes (optional if you prefer a thicker smoothie)

Enjoy the delicious blend of cherries and vanilla in this antioxidant-rich smoothie that's perfect for a healthy start to your day or as a refreshing snack.

 4 servings | 5 minutes | 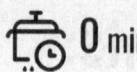 0 minutes

Directions:

1. Combine the frozen cherries, sliced banana, vanilla extract, almond milk, and honey or agave syrup in a blender.
2. Blend at high speed until the mixture becomes smooth and creamy. Add more almond milk to adjust the consistency if the smoothie seems too thick.
3. Taste the smoothie and adjust the sweetness if necessary by adding a bit more honey or agave syrup.
4. If you prefer a colder or thicker smoothie, add a handful of ice cubes to the blender and blend until smooth.
5. Pour the smoothie into glasses and serve immediately.

Nutritional Information: (per serving, approximate) Calories: 140, Protein: 2 g, Carbohydrates: 29 g, Fat: 2 g, Fiber: 3 g, Cholesterol: 0 mg, Sodium: 80 mg, Potassium: 300 mg

Peach Oat Heart-Healthy Smoothie

Ingredients:

- 2 cups frozen peaches
- 1/2 cup rolled oats
- 2 cups almond milk, unsweetened
- 1 banana, sliced
- 1 tablespoon honey or agave syrup (optional, adjust to taste)
- 1 teaspoon vanilla extract
- Ice cubes (optional for a thicker smoothie)

This Peach Oat Heart-Healthy Smoothie combines the natural sweetness of peaches with the wholesome goodness of oats and almond milk for a deliciously creamy drink that supports heart health. Low in cholesterol and rich in fiber, it's an ideal choice for a nutritious and satisfying smoothie.

 4 servings | 5 minutes | 0 minutes

Directions:

For a smooth texture, soak 1/2 cup rolled oats in 1 cup almond milk (or water) and refrigerate overnight to soften. If you're short on time, soak the oats in hot water and let them sit for about 10-15 minutes, then strain off any excess liquid before adding to your smoothie. (Optional)
1. Combine the frozen peaches, rolled oats, almond milk, sliced banana, honey (or agave syrup), and vanilla extract in a blender.
2. Blend at high speed until the mixture is smooth. Add more almond milk to adjust the consistency if the smoothie seems too thick.
3. Taste the smoothie and adjust the sweetness if necessary by adding a bit more honey or agave syrup.
4. If desired, add a handful of ice cubes to the blender and blend again until smooth for a colder and thicker consistency.
5. Pour the smoothie into glasses and serve immediately.

Nutritional Information: (per serving, approximate) Calories: 150, Protein: 3 g, Carbohydrates: 31 g, Fat: 2.5 g, Fiber: 4 g, Cholesterol: 0 mg, Sodium: 80 mg, Potassium: 350 mg

Almond Joyous Smoothie

Ingredients:

- 2 bananas, sliced and frozen
- 1/4 cup almond butter
- 2 tablespoons cocoa powder, unsweetened
- 2 cups coconut milk, unsweetened
- 1/4 cup shredded unsweetened coconut, plus extra for garnish
- 1 tablespoon honey or agave syrup (optional, adjust to taste)
- Ice cubes (optional for a thicker smoothie)

 4 servings  5 minutes  0 minutes

Directions:

1. Combine the frozen banana slices, almond butter, cocoa powder, coconut milk, shredded coconut, and honey (or agave syrup) in a blender.
2. Blend on high speed until the mixture is smooth and creamy. If the smoothie is too thick for your liking, add more coconut milk to adjust the consistency.
3. Taste the smoothie and adjust the sweetness if necessary by adding a bit more honey or agave syrup.
4. You can add a few ice cubes to the blender and grind.
5. Pour the smoothie into glasses and sprinkle grated coconut on top.
6. Now you can enjoy a rich, creamy Almond Joyous smoothie that tastes like your favorite candy bar in a healthy, low-cholesterol form.

This Almond Joyous Smoothie combines the indulgent flavors of almond, coconut, and chocolate in a deliciously healthy drink. It's a joyous treat for any time of day, perfect for satisfying sweet cravings while keeping cholesterol levels in check.

Nutritional Information: (per serving, approximate) Calories: 250, Protein: 4 g, Carbohydrates: 23 g, Fat: 17 g, Fiber: 5 g, Cholesterol: 0 mg, Sodium: 40 mg, Potassium: 400 mg

Turmeric Mango Morning

Ingredients:

- 2 cups frozen mango chunks
- 1 banana, sliced
- 2 cups almond milk, unsweetened
- 1/2 teaspoon ground turmeric
- 1 tablespoon honey or agave syrup (optional, adjust to taste)
- A pinch of black pepper (to enhance turmeric absorption)
- Ice cubes (optional for a colder smoothie)

This Turmeric Mango Morning smoothie blends mango's sweet and tropical flavor with the earthy turmeric spice, enhanced with a touch of black pepper for absorption, creating a deliciously creamy and healthful drink to kickstart your morning.

 4 servings 5 minutes  0 minutes

Directions:

1. In a blender, combine the frozen mango chunks, sliced banana, almond milk, ground turmeric, honey (or agave syrup), and a pinch of black pepper.
2. Blend on high speed until the mixture is smooth and creamy. Add more almond milk to adjust the consistency if the smoothie seems too thick.
3. Taste the smoothie and adjust the sweetness if necessary by adding a bit more honey or agave syrup.
4. If desired, add a handful of ice cubes to the blender and blend until you achieve consistency and temperature.
5. Pour the smoothie into glasses and serve immediately.
6. Enjoy the vibrant and healthful Turmeric Mango Morning smoothie, a perfect way to start your day with a boost of antioxidants and a low-cholesterol treat.

Nutritional Information: (per serving, approximate) Calories: 120, Protein: 2 g, Carbohydrates: 25 g, Fat: 2 g, Fiber: 3 g, Cholesterol: 0 mg, Sodium: 30 mg, Potassium: 300 mg

Kale Pineapple Power Smoothie

Ingredients:

- 2 cups chopped kale, stems removed
- 2 cups frozen pineapple chunks
- 1 banana, sliced
- 2 tablespoons chia seeds
- 2 cups coconut water, unsweetened
- 1 tablespoon honey or agave syrup
(optional, adjust to taste)

This Kale Pineapple Power Smoothie combines the nutritional powerhouse of kale with the sweet, tropical flavor of pineapple, enhanced with chia seeds for added fiber and protein, all in a deliciously hydrating coconut water base. It's a perfect, low-cholesterol choice for a healthy and energizing start to your day or a midday snack.

 4 servings   5 minutes   0 minutes

Directions:

1. Combine the chopped kale, frozen pineapple chunks, sliced banana, chia seeds, and coconut water in a blender.
2. Blend at high speed until the mixture is smooth. Add more coconut water to adjust the consistency if the smoothie seems too thick.
3. Taste the smoothie and adjust the sweetness if necessary by adding a bit more honey or agave syrup.
4. Once the smoothie reaches your desired consistency and taste, pour it into glasses.
5. Serve immediately, offering a nutrient-packed Kale Pineapple Power Smoothie perfect for a refreshing energy boost.

Nutritional Information: (per serving, approximate) Calories: 140, Protein: 3 g, Carbohydrates: 30 g, Fat: 2 g, Fiber: 5 g, Cholesterol: 0 mg, Sodium: 60 mg, Potassium: 450 mg

Peach Yogurt Smoothie

Ingredients:

- 2 cups frozen peach slices
- 1 cup low-fat Greek yogurt, unsweetened
- 1 banana, sliced
- 1 cup almond milk, unsweetened
- 1 tablespoon honey or agave syrup
(optional, adjust to taste)
- Ice cubes (optional for a thicker smoothie)

This Peach Yogurt Smoothie combines the natural sweetness of peaches with the creaminess of Greek yogurt, creating a deliciously smooth drink that's low in cholesterol and high in protein. It's an ideal choice for a healthy and satisfying treat.

 4 servings   5 minutes   0 minutes

Directions:

1. Combine the frozen peach slices, low-fat Greek yogurt, sliced banana, almond milk, and honey (or agave syrup) in a blender.
2. Blend on high speed until the mixture is smooth and creamy. Add more almond milk to adjust the consistency if the smoothie is too thick.
3. Taste the smoothie and adjust the sweetness if necessary by adding a bit more honey or agave syrup.
4. If desired, add a handful of ice cubes to the blender and blend again until you achieve your preferred consistency.
5. Pour the smoothie into glasses and serve immediately.
6. Enjoy the creamy and refreshing Peach Yogurt Smoothie, a perfect blend for a nutritious breakfast or a delightful snack.

Nutritional Information: (per serving, approximate) Calories: 120, Protein: 6 g, Carbohydrates: 22 g, Fat: 1 g, Fiber: 2 g, Cholesterol: 5 mg, Sodium: 60 mg, Potassium: 300 mg

Almond Oat Breakfast Smoothie

Ingredients:

- 1 cup unsweetened almond milk
- 1/2 cup rolled oats
- 1 banana, sliced and frozen
- 1/4 cup raw almonds
- 1 tablespoon chia seeds
- 1 tablespoon honey or maple syrup
- 1/2 teaspoon vanilla extract
- Ice cubes (optional for thicker smoothies)

This Almond Oat Breakfast Smoothie is a hearty and nutritious way to start your day, combining the wholesome goodness of oats and almonds with the natural sweetness of bananas. Packed with fiber, protein, and healthy fats, it's a perfect low-cholesterol option for a quick and satisfying breakfast.

 2 servings   5 minutes 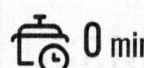 0 minutes

Directions:

1. Place the almond milk and rolled oats in a blender and let them sit for 2-3 minutes, allowing the oats to soften.
2. Add the frozen banana slices, raw almonds, chia seeds, honey (or maple syrup), and vanilla extract to the blender.
3. Blend on high until the mixture is smooth and creamy. Add more almond milk to reach your desired consistency if the smoothie is too thick.
4. If you prefer a colder, thicker smoothie, add a few ice cubes and blend until smooth.
5. Taste and adjust sweetness, if necessary, by adding a bit more honey or maple syrup.
6. Pour the smoothie into glasses and serve immediately.
7. Optional: Garnish with a sprinkle of chia seeds or a few almond slivers.

Nutritional Information: (per serving, approximate) Calories: 280, Protein: 8 g, Carbohydrates: 38 g, Fat: 12 g, Fiber: 7 g, Cholesterol: 0 mg, Sodium: 80 mg, Potassium: 400 mg

Avocado Spinach Omega Boost Smoothie

Ingredients:

- 1 ripe avocado, pitted and scooped out
- 2 cups fresh spinach leaves
- 1 cup unsweetened almond milk
- 1 tablespoon flaxseed meal
- 1/2 cup Greek yogurt, unsweetened (use dairy-free for a vegan option)
- 1 banana, sliced and frozen
- 1 tablespoon honey or maple syrup (optional)
- Ice cubes (optional for a thicker smoothie)

This Avocado Spinach Omega Boost Smoothie is a powerhouse of nutrition, offering a perfect blend of healthy fats from avocado and flaxseed, proteins from Greek yogurt, and vitamins from spinach.

 2 servings   5 minutes   0 minutes

Directions:

1. Combine the avocado, spinach leaves, almond milk, flaxseed meal, and Greek yogurt in a blender.
2. Add the frozen banana slices to the blender. If you're using honey or maple syrup for added sweetness, add it now.
3. Blend on high until the mixture is smooth and creamy. Add more almond milk to adjust the consistency if the smoothie is too thick.
4. For a colder, thicker smoothie, add a few ice cubes and blend again until smooth.
5. Taste the smoothie and adjust the sweetness if needed by adding a bit more honey or maple syrup.
6. Pour the smoothie into glasses and serve immediately for a refreshing, nutrient-packed breakfast.

Nutritional Information: (per serving, approximate) Calories: 220, Protein: 6 g, Carbohydrates: 26 g, Fat: 12 g, Fiber: 7 g, Cholesterol: 0 mg, Sodium: 90 mg, Potassium: 700 mg

Cucumber Melon Hydration Smoothie

Ingredients:

- 1 cup honeydew melon, cubed
- 1 medium cucumber, peeled and sliced
- 1 cup coconut water
- Juice of 1 lime
- A handful of fresh mint leaves
- Ice cubes (optional)

This Cucumber Melon Hydration Smoothie is a light, refreshing drink perfect for starting your day with a low-cholesterol, hydrating boost. Its blend of juicy melon, crisp cucumber, and coconut water is ideal for replenishing fluids and vitamins first thing in the morning.

 2 servings 5 minutes 0 minutes

Directions:

1. Place the cubed honeydew melon and sliced cucumber in the blender.
2. Add the coconut water to the blender for a hydrating base.
3. Squeeze the lime juice directly into the blender.
4. Add the fresh mint leaves for a refreshing flavor.
5. If desired, add a few ice cubes to make the smoothie colder and thicker.
6. Blend on high until all ingredients are thoroughly combined and the smoothie has a smooth, creamy texture.
7. Taste the smoothie, and adjust the sweetness or tartness by adding a bit more lime juice or honeydew melon if needed.
8. Pour the smoothie into glasses and serve immediately for the best flavor and freshness.

Nutritional Information: (per serving, approximate) Calories: 60, Protein: 1 g, Carbohydrates: 14 g, Fat: 0 g, Fiber: 2 g, Cholesterol: 0 mg, Sodium: 30 mg, Potassium: 400 mg

Berry Oatmeal Breakfast Smoothie

Ingredients:

- 1 cup unsweetened almond milk
- 1/2 cup rolled oats
- 1 banana, sliced and frozen
- 1 cup mixed berries (strawberries, blueberries, raspberries), fresh or frozen
- 1 tablespoon chia seeds
- 1 tablespoon honey or maple syrup (optional for sweetness)
- Ice cubes (optional for a thicker smoothie)

This Berry Oatmeal Breakfast Smoothie combines the heart-healthy benefits of oats with the antioxidant-rich flavors of mixed berries for a delicious and nourishing start to your day. Perfect for a low-cholesterol diet, it's a quick and easy way to enjoy a balanced, satisfying breakfast.

 2 servings 5 minutes 0 minutes

Directions:

1. Place the rolled oats in the blender and blend for a few seconds until they become a fine powder.
2. Add the unsweetened almond milk, frozen banana slices, mixed berries, and chia seeds to the blender.
3. If you prefer a sweeter smoothie, add honey or maple syrup to taste.
4. Blend on high until the mixture is smooth and creamy. Add more almond milk to reach your desired consistency if the smoothie is too thick.
5. Add a few ice cubes and blend until smooth for a colder, thicker smoothie.
6. Taste the smoothie and adjust sweetness if necessary by adding a bit more honey or maple syrup.
7. Pour the smoothie into glasses and serve immediately for a refreshing and nutritious breakfast.

Nutritional Information: (per serving, approximate) Calories: 220, Protein: 6 g, Carbohydrates: 42 g, Fat: 4 g, Fiber: 8 g, Cholesterol: 0 mg, Sodium: 80 mg, Potassium: 350 mg

Chocolate Hazelnut Granola Smoothie

 2 servings   5 minutes   0 minutes

Ingredients:

- 1 cup unsweetened almond milk
- 2 tablespoons hazelnut butter
- 1 tablespoon unsweetened cocoa powder
- 1 ripe banana, sliced and frozen
- 1/2 cup low-fat Greek yogurt (use dairy-free yogurt for a vegan option)
- 2 tablespoons honey or maple syrup (adjust to taste)
- 1/2 cup granola (low-sugar, high-fiber variety)
- Ice cubes (optional for a thicker smoothie)

Directions:

1. Combine the almond milk, hazelnut butter, cocoa powder, frozen banana slices, Greek yogurt, and honey or maple syrup in a blender.
2. Blend on high until the mixture is smooth and creamy. Add more almond milk to adjust the consistency if the smoothie is too thick.
3. If desired, add a few ice cubes to the blender and blend until the smoothie reaches your preferred thickness.
4. Taste the smoothie and adjust the sweetness if necessary by adding a bit more honey or maple syrup.
5. Pour the smoothie into glasses, leaving enough room at the top for a layer of granola.
6. Gently spoon the granola over the top of each smoothie.
7. Serve immediately, with a spoon, to enjoy the granola topping.

This Chocolate Hazelnut Granola Smoothie combines the rich flavors of chocolate and hazelnut with the granola crunch, creating a delicious and satisfying low-cholesterol breakfast option. Packed with protein and fiber, it's a perfect way to start your day with energy and nutrients.

Nutritional Information: (per serving, approximate) Calories: 310, Protein: 10 g, Carbohydrates: 42 g, Fat: 12 g, Fiber: 5 g, Cholesterol: 5 mg, Sodium: 120 mg, Potassium: 400 mg

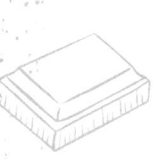
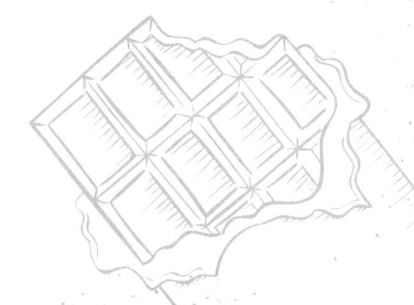

DESERTS AND TREATS:

These recipes are designed to provide delicious, heart-healthy options for those looking to lower their cholesterol levels without sacrificing flavor or indulgence. Each title focuses on natural sweetness, whole grains, and healthy fats.

Orange Chocolate Chip Ricotta Cake

Ingredients:

 6 servings  15 minutes 35 minutes

- 1 1/2 cups all-purpose flour
- 2 teaspoons baking powder
- 1/2 teaspoon salt
- 3/4 cup low-fat ricotta cheese
- 1/2 cup granulated sugar
- 1/4 cup fresh orange juice
- Zest of 1 orange
- 1/2 teaspoon vanilla extract
- 2 large eggs
- 1/4 cup unsweetened applesauce
- 1/2 cup dark chocolate chips

Directions:

1. Preheat the oven to 350°F (175°C). Grease and flour an 8-inch round cake pan.
2. Whisk the flour, baking powder, and salt in a medium bowl. Set aside.
3. In a large bowl, beat the ricotta, sugar, orange juice, orange zest, and vanilla extract until smooth.
4. Add the eggs one at a time, beating well after each addition. Stir in the applesauce.
5. Gradually add the dry ingredients to the ricotta mixture, stirring until combined. Fold in the chocolate chips.
6. Pour the batter into the prepared cake pan and smooth the top with a spatula.
7. Bake for 35 minutes or until a toothpick inserted into the center comes clean.
8. Let the cake cool in the pan for 10 minutes, then transfer to a wire rack to cool completely.

This Orange Chocolate Chip Ricotta Cake offers a delightful combination of citrus and chocolate in a light, low-cholesterol treat. Perfect for any occasion, it's a delicious way to enjoy a healthier dessert option.

Nutritional Information: (per serving, approximate) Calories: 280, Protein: 8 g, Carbohydrates: 42 g, Fat: 9 g, Fiber: 2 g, Cholesterol: 70 mg, Sodium: 300 mg, Potassium: 200 mg

Pear Ginger Crisp with Oat Topping
&
Vanilla Almond Chia Pudding

 4 servings  20 minutes  30 minutes  2 hours

Ingredients:

For the Vanilla Almond Chia Pudding:
- 1/4 cup chia seeds
- 1 cup unsweetened almond milk
- 1 teaspoon vanilla extract
- 1 tablespoon maple syrup

For the Pear Ginger Crisp:
- 4 ripe pears, peeled, cored, and sliced
- 1 tablespoon fresh ginger, grated
- 2 tablespoons honey or agave syrup
- 1/2 teaspoon ground cinnamon

For the Oat Topping:
- 1 cup rolled oats
- 1/4 cup almond flour
- 1/4 cup sliced almonds
- 2 tablespoons coconut oil, melted
- 2 tablespoons maple syrup

Directions:

1. Prepare the Chia Pudding (at least 2 hours before or overnight): In a bowl, mix chia seeds, almond milk, vanilla extract, and maple syrup. Stir well to combine. Let sit for 5 minutes, then stir again to prevent clumping. Cover and refrigerate for at least 2 hours, or overnight, until it reaches a pudding-like consistency.
2. Preheat the oven to 350°F (175°C) while the chia pudding is chilling.
3. Prepare the Pear Ginger Filling: In a mixing bowl, combine the sliced pears, grated ginger, honey (or agave), and cinnamon. Toss to evenly coat and transfer to a baking dish.
4. Make the Oat Topping: In another bowl, combine the rolled oats, almond flour, sliced almonds, melted coconut oil, and maple syrup. Mix until well combined and crumbly. Sprinkle this mixture over the pear filling in the baking dish.
5. Bake for 30 minutes until the topping is golden brown and the pears are tender.
6. To Serve: Spoon the chilled vanilla almond chia pudding into serving glasses or bowls. Top with the warm pear ginger crisp. Optionally, garnish with additional sliced almonds or a drizzle of honey.

Enjoy a prepared dessert that pairs the creamy and cool vanilla almond chia pudding with the warm and spicy pear ginger crisp for a delightful contrast in flavors and textures.

Nutritional Information: (per serving, approximate) Calories: 350, Protein: 8 g, Carbohydrates: 55 g, Fat: 12 g, Fiber: 10 g, Cholesterol: 0 mg, Sodium: 50 mg, Potassium: 400 mg

Oatmeal Berry Crumble Bars

 6 servings  15 minutes  25 minutes

Ingredients:

- 2 cups rolled oats
- 1 cup whole wheat flour
- 1/3 cup brown sugar
- 1/2 teaspoon baking powder
- 1/2 teaspoon cinnamon
- 1/4 teaspoon salt
- 1/2 cup unsweetened applesauce
- 1/4 cup almond milk
- 1 teaspoon vanilla extract
- 2 cups mixed berries (fresh or frozen and thawed)
- 2 tablespoons cornstarch
- 2 tablespoons honey or agave syrup

Directions:

1. Preheat your oven to 375°F (190°C) and line an 8x8 inch baking dish with parchment paper.
2. Mix the rolled oats, whole-wheat flour, brown sugar, baking powder, cinnamon, and salt in a large bowl.
3. Stir in the applesauce, almond milk, and vanilla extract until the mixture is well combined and crumbly.
4. Press about two-thirds of the oat mixture firmly into the bottom of the prepared baking dish to form a crust.
5. In a separate bowl, toss the mixed berries with cornstarch and honey or agave syrup, then spread the berry mixture evenly over the crust.
6. Crumble the remaining oat mixture over the berries.
7. Bake for 25 minutes until the topping is golden brown and the berry filling is bubbling.
8. Let the bars cool completely in the dish on a wire rack before slicing them into squares.

These Oatmeal Berry Crumble Bars offer a delightful balance of sweet and tart flavors with a chewy and crumbly texture. Perfect as a low-cholesterol breakfast or a healthy snack, they're packed with whole grains and fruit, making them a nutritious treat for any time of the day.

Nutritional Information: (per serving, approximate) Calories: 220, Protein: 4 g, Carbohydrates: 44 g, Fat: 3 g, Fiber: 6 g, Cholesterol: 0 mg, Sodium: 100 mg, Potassium: 200 mg

Dark Chocolate Quinoa Truffles

 6 servings 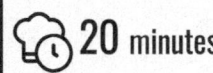 20 minutes  0 minutes 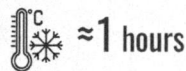 ≈1 hours

Ingredients:

- 1 cup cooked quinoa, cooled
- 1/2 cup dates, pitted
- 1/4 cup unsweetened cocoa powder, plus extra for rolling
- 1/4 cup almond butter
- 1 teaspoon vanilla extract
- A pinch of salt
- 3.5 ounces (100 grams) of dark chocolate, at least 70% cocoa, melted

These Dark Chocolate Quinoa Truffles offer a unique twist on a classic treat, combining quinoa's health benefits with dark chocolate's decadence for a delightful, low-cholesterol indulgence. Perfect for satisfying your sweet tooth more healthily.

Directions:

1.1.Place the cooked quinoa, pitted dates, cocoa powder, almond butter, vanilla extract, and a pinch of salt in a food processor. Blend until the mixture comes together and forms a sticky dough.
2. Transfer the mixture to a bowl. If the mixture is too sticky to handle, refrigerate for about 30 minutes to firm up.
3. Once chilled, roll each portion between your hands to form balls.
4. Dip each ball into the melted dark chocolate, using a fork to turn and coat evenly. Let the excess chocolate drip off before transferring to a parchment-lined tray.
5. Optionally, roll the chocolate-coated truffles in additional cocoa powder for a classic truffle finish.
6. Place the truffles in the refrigerator for at least 1 hour until the chocolate coating is firm.
7. Serve the truffles chilled. Store any leftovers in an airtight container in the refrigerator.

Nutritional Information: (per serving, approximate) Calories: 220, Protein: 5 g, Carbohydrates: 28 g, Fat: 11 g, Fiber: 4 g, Cholesterol: 0 mg, Sodium: 40 mg, Potassium: 300 mg

Spiced Baked Apples with Raisins

Ingredients:

 4 servings  10 minutes  30 minutes

- 4 large apples, such as Fuji or Granny Smith
- 1/4 cup raisins
- 2 tablespoons chopped walnuts (optional)
- 1/2 teaspoon ground cinnamon
- 1/4 teaspoon ground nutmeg (optional)
- 1 tablespoon honey or maple syrup
- 1/2 cup apple juice or water
- 1 teaspoon lemon juice

These Spiced Baked Apples with Raisins are a delicious, low-cholesterol dessert that combines the natural sweetness of apples with the warmth of autumn spices. Easy to prepare and comforting to eat, they make for a perfect healthy treat on a chilly day.

Directions:

1. Preheat your oven to 350°F (175°C). Core the apples, leaving the bottom intact, to create a well in the center of each apple.
2. Mix the raisins, walnuts (if using), cinnamon, and nutmeg in a small bowl. Drizzle the honey or maple syrup over the mixture and stir to combine.
3. Spoon the raisin mixture into the wells of each apple, packing it in tightly.
4. Place the stuffed apples in a baking dish. Mix the apple juice (or water) with lemon juice and pour it into the bottom of the dish around the apples.
5. Bake in the preheated oven for 30 minutes or until the apples are tender when pierced with a fork. Baste the apples occasionally with the liquid from the dish to keep them moist.
6. Serve the baked apples warm, spooning some of the cooking juices over the top of each apple.

Nutritional Information: (per serving, approximate) Calories: 150, Protein: 1 g, Carbohydrates: 37 g, Fat: 1 g, Fiber: 5 g, Cholesterol: 0 mg, Sodium: 10 mg, Potassium: 250 mg

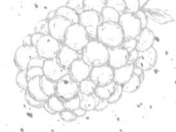

No-Bake Peanut Butter Oat Squares

 6 servings  15 minutes 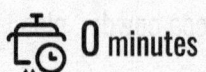 0 minutes 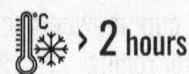 › 2 hours

Ingredients:

- 2 cups rolled oats
- 1 cup natural peanut butter (unsweetened and unsalted)
- 1/2 cup honey or agave syrup
- 1/4 cup chopped dark chocolate or dark chocolate chips (optional)
- 1 teaspoon vanilla extract

Directions:

1. Line an 8x8 inch square baking dish with parchment paper, leaving some overhang on the sides for easy removal.
2. Combine the rolled oats and natural peanut butter in a large mixing bowl.
3. In a small saucepan over low heat, gently warm the honey or agave syrup until it becomes more fluid. Remove from heat and stir in the vanilla extract.
4. Pour the warm honey mixture over the oats and peanut butter. Mix well until all the oats are coated and the mixture is evenly combined.
5. If using, fold the chopped dark chocolate or chocolate chips.
6. Transfer the mixture to the prepared baking dish. Press down firmly with a spatula or your hands to create an even layer.
7. Chill in the refrigerator for at least 2 hours or until the mixture is firm and set.
8. Once set, use the parchment paper to lift the square out of the dish. Cut into 6 equal squares or bars.
9. Serve chilled. Store any leftovers in an airtight container in the refrigerator.

These No-Bake Peanut Butter Oat Squares are a delicious, low-cholesterol treat perfect for satisfying your sweet tooth. Made with simple, wholesome ingredients, they offer a healthier alternative to traditional desserts and snacks.

Nutritional Information: (per serving, approximate) Calories: 320, Protein: 10 g, Carbohydrates: 36 g, Fat: 16 g, Fiber: 4 g, Cholesterol: 0 mg, Sodium: 50 mg, Potassium: 300 mg

Blueberry Lemon Chia Seed Cake

 6 servings |  15 minutes |  35 minutes

Ingredients:

- 1 1/2 cups whole wheat flour
- 1/2 cup almond flour
- 3 tablespoons chia seeds
- 2 teaspoons baking powder
- 1/2 teaspoon salt
- 1/2 cup unsweetened applesauce
- 1/2 cup almond milk, unsweetened
- 1/2 cup honey or agave syrup
- Zest of 1 lemon (optional)
- 1/4 cup lemon juice
- 1/2 teaspoon vanilla extract
- 1 cup fresh or frozen blueberries

Directions:

1. Preheat your oven to 350°F (175°C). Grease and flour an 8-inch round cake pan.
2. Whisk whole-wheat flour, almond flour, chia seeds, baking powder, and salt in a large bowl.
3. In another bowl, mix the unsweetened applesauce, almond milk, honey (or agave syrup), lemon zest, lemon juice, and vanilla extract until well combined.
4. Gradually add the wet and dry ingredients, stirring until combined. Be careful not to overmix.
5. Gently fold in the blueberries, being careful not to crush them.
6. Pour the batter into the prepared cake pan and smooth the top with a spatula.
7. Bake in the preheated oven for 35 minutes or until a toothpick inserted into the center of the cake comes out clean.
8. Let the cake cool in the pan for 10 minutes, then transfer it to a wire rack to cool completely.

This Blueberry Lemon Chia Seed Cake is a moist, flavorful, and low-cholesterol dessert that combines the tangy taste of lemon with the sweetness of blueberries, complemented by the nutritional boost of chia seeds. Perfect for a healthy treat or a special occasion.

Nutritional Information: (per serving, approximate) Calories: 280, Protein: 6 g, Carbohydrates: 46 g, Fat: 8 g, Fiber: 6 g, Cholesterol: 0 mg, Sodium: 200 mg, Potassium: 150 mg

Berry Cashew Cream Parfait

 4 servings |  15 minutes | 0 minutes

Ingredients:

- 1 cup raw cashews, soaked overnight or at least 4 hours
- 1/4 cup almond milk, unsweetened
- 2 tablespoons honey or agave syrup
- 1 teaspoon vanilla extract
- 2 cups mixed berries (strawberries, blueberries, raspberries)
- 1/4 cup low-sugar granola (a crunchy mix of oat flakes, nuts, seeds, and a sweet binding agent. Look for a granola with a high fiber content and minimal added sugars)

Directions:

1. After soaking, drain and rinse the cashews. Transfer them to a high-speed blender.
2. Add almond milk, honey (or agave syrup), and vanilla extract to the blender with the cashews.
3. Blend on high until the mixture is completely smooth and creamy. Add a little more almond milk if needed to adjust the consistency.
4. To assemble the parfaits, spoon a layer of the cashew cream into the bottom of the serving glasses.
5. Add a layer of mixed berries over the cashew cream.
6. Sprinkle a layer of low-sugar granola over the berries. The granola will add a delightful crunch and fiber without adding too much sugar to the parfait.
7. Repeat the layering process until the glasses are filled to the top, finishing with a layer of berries.
8. Optionally, top each parfait with a final sprinkle of granola for presentation.
9. Refrigerate the parfaits for at least 30 minutes to allow the flavors to blend.
10. Serve chilled as a nutritious and delicious dessert or breakfast option.

Choosing low-sugar granola for this Berry Cashew Cream Parfait ensures you maintain the low cholesterol benefits of the dish while adding texture and nutritional value. Look for granolas that use small amounts of natural sweeteners like honey or maple syrup and those rich in nuts and seeds for extra protein and healthy fats.

This Berry Cashew Cream Parfait is a delightful, cholesterol-free treat that combines the creamy richness of cashew cream with the fresh sweetness of mixed berries, making it a perfect dessert or breakfast option for those following a low-cholesterol diet.

Nutritional Information: (per serving, approximate) Calories: 280, Protein: 7 g, Carbohydrates: 34 g, Fat: 15 g, Fiber: 5 g, Cholesterol: 0 mg, Sodium: 25 mg, Potassium: 320 mg

Zucchini Brownies with Natural Sweetener

 6 servings |  15 minutes | 25 minutes

Ingredients:

- 1 cup whole wheat flour
- 1/3 cup unsweetened cocoa powder
- 1 1/2 teaspoons baking soda
- 1/4 teaspoon salt
- 1/2 cup unsweetened applesauce
- 1/4 cup vegetable oil
- 3/4 cup pure maple syrup or honey (as a natural sweetener alternative to granulated sugar)
- 1 teaspoon vanilla extract
- 2 cups grated zucchini, excess water squeezed out
- 1/2 cup chopped walnuts (optional)

Directions:

1. Preheat your oven to 350°F (175°C). Grease and flour in an 8x8-inch baking pan.
2. Whisk the whole wheat flour, cocoa powder, baking soda, and salt in a mixing bowl.
3. In another large bowl, blend the applesauce, vegetable oil, maple syrup (or honey), and vanilla extract until well combined.
4. Fold the grated zucchini and walnuts (if using) into the wet ingredients until evenly incorporated.
5. Gradually mix the dry and wet ingredients, stirring until combined to avoid overmixing.
6. Transfer the batter to the prepared baking pan, smoothing it into an even layer.
7. Bake in the preheated oven for about 25 minutes or until a toothpick inserted into the center is clean.
8. Let the brownies cool in the pan before cutting them into squares for serving.

These Zucchini Brownies offer a delicious, low-cholesterol dessert option that incorporates the moisture and nutrition of zucchini into a classic treat. Whole-wheat flour and unsweetened applesauce provide a healthier alternative to traditional brownie recipes.

Nutritional Information: (per serving, approximate, with maple syrup) Calories: 300, Protein: 4 g, Carbohydrates: 52 g, Fat: 10 g, Fiber: 3 g, Cholesterol: 0 mg, Sodium: 270 mg, Potassium: 250 mg.

Carrot Cake Oatmeal Cookies

 6 servings    15 minutes   12 minutes

Ingredients:

- 1 cup rolled oats
- 3/4 cup whole wheat flour
- 1 1/2 teaspoons baking powder
- 1 1/2 teaspoons ground cinnamon
- 1/4 teaspoon ground nutmeg
- 1/4 teaspoon salt
- 1/4 cup unsweetened applesauce
- 1/4 cup honey or maple syrup
- 1 large egg
- 1 teaspoon vanilla extract
- 1 cup grated carrots
- 1/2 cup raisins

Directions:

1. Preheat your oven to 350°F (175°C) and line a baking sheet with parchment paper.
2. Whisk the rolled oats, whole wheat flour, baking powder, cinnamon, nutmeg, and salt in a large bowl.
3. In another bowl, mix the unsweetened applesauce, honey (or maple syrup), egg, and vanilla extract until well combined.
4. Add the wet ingredients to the dry ingredients, stirring until combined without overmixing.
5. Fold the grated carrots and raisins gently until evenly distributed throughout the batter.
6. Drop tablespoon-sized portions of the dough onto the prepared baking sheet, spacing them about 2 inches apart. Flatten them slightly with the back of the spoon.
7. Bake in the preheated oven for 12 minutes or until the edges of the cookies are golden brown.
8. Allow the cookies to cool on the baking sheet for 5 minutes before transferring them to a wire rack to cool completely.

These Carrot Cake Oatmeal Cookies offer a wholesome, low-cholesterol treat that combines the classic flavors of carrot cake with the hearty texture of oatmeal cookies. Perfect for a healthy snack or dessert that doesn't compromise on taste.

Nutritional Information: (per serving, approximate) Calories: 180, Protein: 4 g, Carbohydrates: 36 g, Fat: 2 g, Fiber: 4 g, Cholesterol: 31 mg, Sodium: 150 mg, Potassium: 200 mg

Berry Almond Crisp

 4 servings    15 minutes    30 minutes

Ingredients:

- 4 cups mixed berries (fresh or frozen)
- 1 tablespoon lemon juice
- 1 tablespoon cornstarch
- 1/2 cup rolled oats
- 1/2 cup almond flour
- 1/4 cup sliced almonds
- 1/4 cup honey or maple syrup
- 1/4 cup unsweetened applesauce
- 1 teaspoon ground cinnamon
- A pinch of salt

Directions:

1. Preheat your oven to 375°F (190°C). Lightly grease an 8-inch square baking dish.
2. Toss the mixed berries with lemon juice and cornstarch in a large bowl. Spread the berry mixture evenly in the bottom of the prepared baking dish.
3. In another bowl, combine the rolled oats, almond flour, sliced almonds, honey (or maple syrup), unsweetened applesauce, ground cinnamon, and a pinch of salt. Mix until the mixture resembles coarse crumbs.
4. Evenly distribute the oat mixture over the berries in the baking dish.
5. Bake in the preheated oven for 30 minutes or until the topping is golden brown and the berry filling is bubbling.
6. Let the crisp cool slightly before serving. It can be served warm or at room temperature.
7. Optional: Serve with a dollop of low-fat Greek yogurt or a scoop of low-fat vanilla ice cream for an extra treat.

This Berry Almond Crisp offers a delicious, heart-healthy dessert perfect for satisfying your sweet tooth without the added cholesterol. The combination of juicy berries, crunchy almonds, and a hint of cinnamon makes for a delightful treat.

Nutritional Information: (per serving, approximate) Calories: 280, Protein: 6 g, Carbohydrates: 46 g, Fat: 10 g, Fiber: 7 g, Cholesterol: 0 mg, Sodium: 50 mg, Potassium: 200 mg

Avocado Chocolate Mousse

Ingredients:

- 2 ripe avocados, peeled and pitted
- 1/4 cup unsweetened cocoa powder
- 1/4 cup honey or maple syrup (adjust to taste)
- 1/2 teaspoon vanilla extract
- A pinch of salt
- 1/4 cup almond milk, unsweetened (adjust for desired consistency)

This Avocado Chocolate Mousse is a luxurious, low-cholesterol dessert that combines the creamy texture of ripe avocados with rich cocoa powder for a healthy twist on traditional chocolate mousse. Perfect for satisfying your sweet tooth while keeping health in mind.

 4 servings  10 minutes  0 minutes

Directions:

1. Place the avocados in a blender or food processor.
2. Add the cocoa powder, honey (or maple syrup), vanilla extract, and a pinch of salt.
3. Start blending on low, gradually increasing to high speed until the mixture is completely smooth.
4. While blending, slowly add almond milk until you reach your desired consistency. The mixture should be creamy and smooth.
5. Taste the mousse and adjust the sweetness if necessary by adding a bit more honey or maple syrup.
6. Once fully blended, divide the mousse into serving dishes.
7. Refrigerate the mousse for at least 1 hour to chill and set.
8. Serve chilled, optionally garnished with fresh berries, a sprinkle of cocoa powder, or shaved dark chocolate.

Nutritional Information: (per serving, approximate) Calories: 230, Protein: 3 g, Carbohydrates: 27 g, Fat: 14 g, Fiber: 7 g, Cholesterol: 0 mg, Sodium: 60 mg, Potassium: 487 mg

Apricot Almond Energy Bites

Ingredients:

- 1 cup dried apricots
- 1/2 cup raw almonds
- 1/4 cup unsweetened shredded coconut
- 1 tablespoon chia seeds
- 1 tablespoon honey or maple syrup
- 1 teaspoon vanilla extract
- A pinch of salt

These Apricot Almond Energy Bites are a delicious, low-cholesterol snack packed with natural sweetness from apricots and a crunchy texture from almonds. They're perfect for a quick energy boost before a workout or as a healthy snack on the go.

 4 servings  15 minutes  0 minutes

Directions:

1. Place the dried apricots and raw almonds in a food processor and pulse until they are finely chopped and begin to stick together.
2. Add the unsweetened shredded coconut, chia seeds, honey (or maple syrup), vanilla extract, and a pinch of salt to the food processor.
3. Pulse several more times until all ingredients are well combined and the mixture sticks together when pressed between your fingers.
4. Scoop out tablespoon-sized amounts of the mixture and roll into balls between your hands. If the mixture is too sticky, slightly wet your hands before rolling.
5. Place the formed energy bites on a plate or baking sheet lined with parchment paper.
6. Refrigerate the energy bites to set and become firm for at least 1 hour.
7. Store the energy bites in an airtight container in the refrigerator for up to a week or in the freezer for more extended storage.

Nutritional Information: (per serving, approximate) Calories: 220, Protein: 5 g, Carbohydrates: 30 g, Fat: 10 g, Fiber: 5 g, Cholesterol: 0 mg, Sodium: 25 mg, Potassium: 400 mg

Cacao Nib Coconut Energy Balls

 4 servings  15 minutes  0 minutes

Ingredients:

- 1 cup dates, pitted
- 1/2 cup raw almonds
- 1/2 cup shredded unsweetened coconut
- 1/4 cup cacao nibs
- 1 tablespoon chia seeds
- 1 tablespoon coconut oil, melted
- 1 teaspoon vanilla extract
- A pinch of salt

Directions:

1. Place the dates in a food processor and pulse a few times until they form a sticky paste.
2. Add the raw almonds to the processor and pulse until the almonds are finely chopped and well incorporated with the date paste.
3. Add the shredded coconut, cacao nibs, chia seeds, melted coconut oil, vanilla extract, and a pinch of salt to the food processor.
4. Pulse the mixture several times until all ingredients are well combined and the mixture sticks together when pressed.
5. Scoop out tablespoon-sized portions of the mixture and roll them between your palms to form balls.
6. If the mixture is too sticky, slightly wet your hands before rolling.
7. Place the formed energy balls on a plate or tray lined with parchment paper.
8. Refrigerate the energy balls for at least 1 hour to firm up before serving.
9. Store the energy balls in an airtight container in the refrigerator for up to a week or in the freezer for more extended storage.

These Cacao Nib Coconut Energy Balls are a delicious, low-cholesterol snack packed with healthy fats, fiber, and antioxidants. Perfect for a quick energy boost or a satisfying sweet treat without the guilt.

Nutritional Information: (per serving, approximate) Calories: 280, Protein: 5 g, Carbohydrates: 30 g, Fat: 17 g, Fiber: 7 g, Cholesterol: 0 mg, Sodium: 25 mg, Potassium: 300 mg

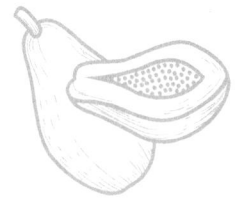

No-Bake Oatmeal Cocoa Balls

 **4** servings    **10** minutes    **0** minutes

Ingredients:

- 1 cup rolled oats
- 1/4 cup unsweetened cocoa powder
- 1/2 cup natural peanut butter (unsalted and unsweetened)
- 1/3 cup honey or agave syrup
- 1 teaspoon vanilla extract
- A pinch of salt
- Optional: 1/4 cup mini dark chocolate chips (for added texture and flavor)

Directions:

1. Combine the rolled oats and unsweetened cocoa powder in a large mixing bowl.
2. Add the natural peanut butter, honey (or agave syrup), vanilla extract, and a pinch of salt to the oat mixture.
3. Mix well until all ingredients are thoroughly combined. If the mixture seems too dry, add more peanut butter or honey to achieve a sticky consistency that holds together when pressed.
4. If using, fold in the mini dark chocolate chips.
5. Wet your hands slightly and scoop out tablespoon-sized portions of the mixture.
6. Roll the portions into balls between your palms. If the mixture sticks to your hands, keep them wet by dipping them in water as needed.
7. Place the rolled balls on a plate or baking sheet lined with parchment paper.
8. Refrigerate the oatmeal cocoa balls for at least 1 hour to set and firm up.
9. Serve chilled. Store any leftovers in an airtight container in the refrigerator for up to a week.

These No-Bake Oatmeal Cocoa Balls are a convenient and delicious low-cholesterol snack, packed with the goodness of oats and the rich flavor of cocoa. Perfect for a quick energy boost or a healthy treat on the go.

Nutritional Information: (per serving, approximate) Calories: 280, Protein: 8 g, Carbohydrates: 34 g, Fat: 14 g, Fiber: 5 g, Cholesterol: 0 mg, Sodium: 75 mg, Potassium: 300 mg

Lemon Ginger Poached Pears

🍽 4 servings | 🕙 10 minutes | ⏲ 25 minutes

Ingredients:

- 4 ripe pears, peeled, halved, and cored
- 4 cups water
- 1/2 cup honey or agave syrup
- Juice of 1 lemon
- 2-inch piece of fresh ginger, peeled and thinly sliced
- 1 vanilla bean, split lengthwise (or 1 teaspoon vanilla extract)
- Optional for garnish: a sprinkle of cinnamon or mint leaves

Directions:

1. Combine water, honey (or agave syrup), lemon juice, sliced ginger, and vanilla bean (or vanilla extract) in a large saucepan.
2. Bring the mixture to a simmer over medium heat, stirring until the honey fully dissolves.
3. Carefully add the pear halves to the simmering liquid. The pears should be mostly submerged. If necessary, add a bit more water to cover.
4. Reduce the heat to low, cover the saucepan, and let the pears poach gently for 20-25 minutes until they are tender when pierced with a fork but not falling apart.
5. Once the pears are poached, use a slotted spoon to carefully transfer them to serving dishes.
6. Increase the heat to medium-high and bring the poaching liquid to a boil. Let it reduce by half, taking about 10-15 minutes, until slightly thickening into a syrup.
7. Strain the reduced syrup to remove the ginger slices and vanilla bean, then pour it over the poached pears.
8. Garnish with a sprinkle of cinnamon or fresh mint leaves if desired.
9 Serve the poached pears warm or allow them to cool to room temperature.

These Lemon Ginger Poached Pears offer a light and refreshing dessert that is low in cholesterol and fully flavored. The combination of lemon and ginger provides a vibrant taste that perfectly complements the pears' sweetness.

Nutritional Information: (per serving, approximate) Calories: 220, Protein: 1 g, Carbohydrates: 58 g, Fat: 0 g, Fiber: 5 g, Cholesterol: 0 mg, Sodium: 10 mg, Potassium: 210 mg

Almond Flour Blueberry Muffins

 6 servings | 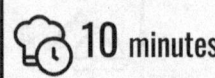 10 minutes |  20 minutes

Ingredients:

- 2 cups almond flour
- 1/2 teaspoon baking soda
- 1/4 teaspoon salt
- 3 large eggs
- 1/4 cup honey or agave syrup
- 1 teaspoon vanilla extract
- 1/4 cup unsweetened almond milk
- 1 tablespoon lemon zest (optional)
- 1 cup fresh blueberries

Directions:

1. Preheat your oven to 350°F (175°C). Line a muffin tin with 6 paper liners or lightly grease with cooking spray.
2. Whisk almond flour, baking soda, and salt in a large bowl.
3. In a separate bowl, beat the eggs lightly. Stir in honey (or agave syrup), vanilla extract, almond milk, and lemon zest until well combined.
4. Gradually add the wet and dry ingredients, stirring until combined. Avoid overmixing.
5. Gently fold in the blueberries, ensuring they are evenly distributed throughout the batter.
6. Divide the batter evenly among the prepared muffin cups, filling each about 3/4 full.
7. Bake in the preheated oven for 18-20 minutes, until the muffins are golden on top and a toothpick inserted into the center comes clean.
8. Allow the muffins to cool in the pan for 5 minutes before transferring them to a wire rack to cool completely.

These Almond Flour Blueberry Muffins are a delicious, low-cholesterol treat perfect for breakfast or a snack. Made with nutrient-dense almond flour and naturally sweetened with honey, they offer a healthier alternative to traditional muffin recipes without sacrificing flavor.

Nutritional Information: (per serving, approximate) Calories: 280, Protein: 9 g, Carbohydrates: 21 g, Fat: 19 g, Fiber: 4 g, Cholesterol: 93 mg, Sodium: 210 mg, Potassium: 100 mg

Fresh Fruit Salad

  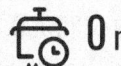

4 servings | **15** minutes | **0** minutes

Ingredients:

- 1 cup strawberries, hulled and halved
- 1 cup blueberries
- 1 cup raspberries
- 1 large mango, peeled and diced
- 2 kiwis, peeled and sliced
- 1/2 cup orange juice
- 2 tablespoons honey or agave syrup
- 1 tablespoon fresh lime juice
- 1/4 cup fresh mint leaves, finely chopped (optional)

Directions:

1. Combine the strawberries, blueberries, raspberries, diced mango, and sliced kiwis in a large mixing bowl.
2. In a small bowl, whisk together the orange juice, honey (or agave syrup), and lime juice until well combined.
3. Pour the orange juice mixture over the mixed fruit, gently tossing to coat all the fruits evenly.
4. Sprinkle the finely chopped mint leaves over the fruit salad and gently toss to distribute the mint.
5. Cover the bowl with plastic wrap and refrigerate the fruit salad for at least 30 minutes to allow the flavors to meld together.
6. Before serving, gently stir the fruit salad to mix up any juices that have settled at the bottom.
7. Serve the fruit salad chilled, garnished with additional mint leaves if desired.

This Fresh Fruit Salad with Mint is a vibrant, low-cholesterol dish perfect for a healthy dessert or refreshing snack. Bursting with a variety of fresh fruits and accented with the bright flavor of mint, it's a delicious way to enjoy the natural sweetness of the fruit.

Nutritional Information: (per serving, approximate) Calories: 150, Protein: 2 g, Carbohydrates: 37 g, Fat: 0.5 g, Fiber: 5 g, Cholesterol: 0 mg, Sodium: 5 mg, Potassium: 350 mg

Conclusion

As we conclude this journey through the world of low-cholesterol cooking, I hope you've discovered that embracing a heart-healthy diet doesn't mean sacrificing flavor or variety. Each recipe within these pages has been crafted to promote your health and please your palate. Remember, managing cholesterol levels is not just about avoiding certain foods; it's about making informed, balanced choices and embracing a lifestyle that contributes to your overall well-being.

I encourage you to experiment with the recipes, adapt them to your tastes, and incorporate them into your daily life. Cooking is an art and a science, and each meal is an opportunity to nourish your body and soul. Let these recipes be a starting point for your culinary adventures and a stepping stone towards a healthier life.

It's important to remember that while diet plays a crucial role in managing cholesterol, it works best in concert with other lifestyle changes, including regular physical activity, maintaining a healthy weight, and avoiding smoking. Always consult with healthcare professionals to tailor a plan that's right for you.

Finally, remember that change doesn't happen overnight. Be patient with yourself and recognize each small step forward as progress. Your journey to a healthier heart is not just about the food on your plate; it's about making sustainable changes that enhance your life.

Thank you for allowing me to be a part of your journey to better health.

author **Rowena Payne**

30-DAY MEAL PLAN

No	BREAKFAST	LUNCH	DINNER
1	Pear & Walnut Overnight Oats Chol: 5mg, Cal: 250, p.12	Chicken and Vegetable Kebabs Chol:55 mg, Cal: 220, p.58 + Whole Wheat Couscous with Herbs and Lemon Chol:0 mg, Cal: 230, p.38	Tuna and White Bean Salad with Lemon Vinaigrette Chol: 30 mg, Cal: 280 p.76
2	Mediterranean Veggie Breakfast Bowl Chol: 0 mg, Cal: 250, p.12	Baked Cod with Tomato and Basil Chol: 60 mg, Cal: 200, p.41 + Whole-Grain Brown Rice Pilaf Chol: 0 mg, Cal: 220, p.35	Turkey and Cranberry Spinach Salad Chol:3 0 mg, Cal: 280, p.80
3	Almond Oat Breakfast Smoothie Chol: 0 mg, Cal: 280, p.111	Lentil and Spinach Soup Chol: 0 mg, Cal: 220, p.26 + Grilled Chicken, Avocado, and Mixed Greens Salad Chol: 65 mg, Cal: 290, p.83	Fish Tacos with Cabbage Slaw Chol: 50 mg, Cal: 280, p.44
4	Baked Avocado Eggs with Bell Pepper Chol: 185 mg, Cal: 220, p.13	Chicken Cacciatore with Whole Wheat Pasta Chol: 65 mg, Cal: 350, p.49 + Salad with Lemon-Olive Dressing Chol: 0 mg, Cal: 120, p.84	Lentil and Roasted Red Pepper Salad Chol: 8 mg, Cal: 290, p.75
5	Pumpkin Spice Quinoa Porridge Chol: 0 mg, Cal: 210, p.14	Shrimp Stir-Fry with Vegetables Chol:180 mg, Cal: 250, p.41 + Spinach, Avocado, and Pomegranate Salad Chol: 0 mg, Cal: 230, p.82	Grilled Chicken, Avocado, and Mixed Greens Salad Chol: 65 mg, Cal: 290, p.83
6	Apple Cinnamon Baked Oatmeal Chol: 30 mg, Cal: 220, p.15	Beef and Mushroom Stroganoff Chol: 85 mg, Cal: 390, p.52 + Fresh Vegetable Salad with Dijon Dressing Chol: 0 mg, Cal: 120, p.85	Mushroom and Barley Risotto Chol: 5 mg, Cal: 350, p.40
7	Apple Barley and Berry Breakfast Salad Chol: 0 mg, Cal: 220, p.15	Chicken Fajitas + Greek Yogurt Sauce with Avocado Cream Chol: 65 mg, Cal: 430, p.50,51	Crispy Tofu and Noodle Salad Chol: 0mg, Cal: 360 p.81

8	**Avocado Spinach Omega Boost Smoothie** Chol: 0 mg, Cal: 220, p.111	**Turkey and Barley Stew** Chol: 50mg, Cal: 300, p.30 + **Tomato, Basil, and Mozzarella Caprese Salad** Chol: 45mg, Cal: 220 p.78	**Spinach and Feta Stuffed Chicken** Chol: 85 mg, Cal: 250, p.63
9	**Whole-Grain Waffles with Blueberry Compote** Chol: 50 mg, Cal: 300, p.16	**Lemon-Garlic Tilapia with Asparagus** Chol: 60 mg, Cal: 220, p.42 + **Mediterranean Quinoa Salad** Chol: 5 mg, Cal: 220, p.70	**Grilled Chicken and Mango Salad** Chol: 40 mg, Cal: 250, p.69
10	**Mediterranean Chickpea Salad** Chol: 8mg, Cal: 330, p.71	**Lean Beef and Vegetable Soup** Chol: 50mg, Cal: 250, p.30 + **Arugula and Pear Salad with Lemon Dressing** Chol: 4mg, Cal: 180, p.74	**Grilled Chicken with Quinoa and Spinach Salad** Chol: 65mg, Cal: 350, p.81
11	**Smoked Salmon and Avocado on Whole-Grain Bagel** Chol: 50mg, Cal: 400, p.18	**Pork Chops with Apple Cider Vinegar Sauce** Chol: 65mg, Cal: 310, p.55 + **Sautéed Spinach with Garlic** Chol: 0mg, Cal: 50, p.35	**Cauliflower Steak with Herb Sauce** Chol: 0mg, Cal: 140, p.79
12	**Cranberry Orange Quinoa and Millet Granola** Chol: 0mg, Cal: 300, p.18	**Herb-Crusted Halibut with Roasted Vegetables** Chol: 55mg, Cal: 280, p.43 + **Garlic and Herb Roasted Potatoes** Chol: 0mg, Cal: 200, p.39	**Roasted Duck Breast (Skinless) with Pomegranate Glaze and Quinoa Salad** Chol: 55mg, Cal: 400, p.66
13	**Banana and Walnut Whole-Grain Muffins** Chol: 60mg, Cal: 310, p.19	**Chicken and Vegetable Soup** Chol: 50mg, Cal: 180, p.29 + **Spinach and Strawberry Salad with Balsamic Glaze** Chol: 6mg, Cal: 280, p.63	**Creamy Avocado Pasta with Cherry Tomatoes and Spinach** Chol: 0mg, Cal: 330, p.80
14	**Zucchini and Carrot Fritters with Yogurt Dip** Chol: 95mg, Cal: 160, p.20	**Lean Beef and Broccoli Stir-Fry** Chol: 55mg, Cal: 160, p.56 + **Quinoa Tabbouleh** Chol: 0mg, Cal: 220, p.34	Stuffed Portobello Mushrooms with Spinach and Pecans Chol: 4mg, Cal: 200, p.84
15	**Veggie-Stuffed Breakfast Bell Peppers** Chol: 185mg, Cal: 150, p.19	**Pan-Seared Trout with Almond Butter** Chol: 85mg, Cal: 330 p.43 + **Steamed Broccoli with Lemon Zest** Chol:0 mg, Cal:70, p.34	**Beef Stir-Fry with Bell Peppers and Snow Peas** Chol: 50mg, Cal: 300, p.67

16	**Sweet Potato and Black Bean Breakfast Burrito** Chol: 15mg, Cal: 350 p.21	**Balsamic Glazed Pork Tenderloin** Chol: 70mg, Cal: 240, p.57 + **Tomato, Basil, and Mozzarella Caprese Salad** Chol: 45mg, Cal: 220 p.78	**Seafood Paella with Brown Rice** Chol: 120mg, Cal: 350 p.42
17	**Brown Rice Tuna and Carrot Balls** Chol: 15 mg, Cal: 180, p.22	**Mushroom Barley Soup** Chol: 0 mg, Cal: 250, p.28 + **Whole Grain Garlic Herb Bread** Chol: 0 mg, Cal: 150, p.25	**Baked Cod with Tomato and Basil** Chol: 60 mg, Cal: 200, p.41
18	**Baked Eggplant and Zucchini Casserole** Chol: 10 mg, Cal: 150, p.22	**Baked Haddock with Creamy Dill Sauce** Chol: 80 mg, Cal: 180, p.44 + **Quinoa Tabbouleh** Chol: 0 mg, Cal: 220, p.34	**Vegan Mushroom Risotto** Chol: 0 mg, Cal: 310, p.99
19	**Chocolate Hazelnut Granola Smoothie** Chol: 5 mg, Cal: 310, p.113	**Minestrone with Whole-Grain Pasta** Chol: 0 mg, Cal: 260, p.28 + **Rosemary Garlic Roasted Turkey Breast** Chol: 85 mg, Cal: 230, p.51	**Tuna and White Bean Salad with Lemon Vinaigrette** Chol: 30 mg, Cal: 280 p.76
20	**Mediterranean Chickpea and Avocado Salad** Chol:0 mg, Cal: 250, p.24	**Chicken Piccata with Capers** Chol: 65mg, Cal: 230, p.53 + **Broccoli and Almond Salad with Yogurt Dressing** Chol: 3mg, Cal: 150, p.78	**Mushroom and Barley Stew** Chol:0 mg, Cal: 220, p.93
21	**Sun-dried Tomato and Spinach Omelet** Chol: 0 mg, Cal: 100, p.24	**Shrimp and Vegetable Miso Soup** Chol: 85 mg, Cal: 100, p.32 + **Cucumber Sesame Salad** Chol: 0 mg, Cal: 70, p.82	**Grilled Chicken, Avocado, and Mixed Greens Salad** Chol: 65 mg, Cal: 290, p.83
22	**Roasted Vegetable Breakfast Hash** Chol: 0 mg, Cal: 200, p.25	**Baked Turkey Meatballs with Tomato Basil Sauce** Chol: 110 mg, Cal: 320,p.59 + **Garlic and Herb Roasted Potatoes** Chol: 0 mg, Cal: 200, p.39	**Roasted Vegetable Paella** Chol: 0 mg, Cal: 320, p.98
23	**Spinach and Feta Breakfast Burrito** Chol: 195 mg, Cal: 280, p.14	**Orange-Glazed Salmon with Asparagus** Chol: 0 mg, Cal: 200, p.45 + **Whole Wheat Couscous with Herbs and Lemon** Chol: 0 mg, Cal: 230, p.38	**Turkey and Cranberry Spinach Salad** Chol: 30 mg, Cal: 280, p.80

24	**Mediterranean Quinoa Salad** Chol: 0 mg, Cal: 270, p.70	**Turkey & Vegetable Stir-Fry with Homemade Stir-Fry Sauce** Chol: 60 mg, Cal: 270, p.60	**Chicken Tikka Masala with Cauliflower Rice** Chol: 75 mg, Cal: 350, p.67
25	**Peach Oat Heart-Healthy Smoothie** Chol: 0mg, Cal: 150, p.108	**Honey Garlic Baked Scallops** Chol: 35mg, Cal: 220, p.46 + **Barley and Roasted Vegetable Pilaf** Chol: 0mg, Cal: 220, p.37	**Ratatouille with Crispy Polenta** Chol: 0mg, Cal: 280, p.97
26	**Baked Sweet Potato and Kale Hash** Chol: 0mg, Cal: 200, p.17	**Balsamic Glazed Chicken Drumsticks** Chol: 100mg, Cal: 200, p.61 + **Roasted Brussels Sprouts with Lemon** Chol: 0 mg, Cal: 100, p.37	**Poached Salmon Salad with Dill and Cucumber** Chol: 60mg, Cal: 280, p.79
27	**Whole-Grain Toast with Ricotta and Sliced Strawberries** Chol: 20 mg, Cal: 210, p.13	**Hearty Vegetable Stew** Chol: 0mg, Cal: 200, p.27 + **Grilled Chicken and Mango Salad** Chol: 40mg, Cal: 250, p.73	**Mediterranean Chickpea Salad** Chol: 8mg, Cal: 330, p.71
28	**Savory Mushroom and Zucchini Pancakes** Chol: 95 mg, Cal: 140, p.16	**Mediterranean Turkey Stuffed Peppers** Chol: 60 mg, Cal: 320, p.63	**Pan-Seared Cod with Parsley Cauliflower Rice** Chol: 60 mg, Cal: 250, p.48
29	**Blueberry and Lemon Ricotta Pancakes** Chol: 55 mg, Cal: 220, p.23	**Grilled Mahi-Mahi (dorado) with Mango Salsa** Chol: 100 mg, Cal: 240, p.46 + **Whole Wheat Couscous with Herbs and Lemon** Chol: 0 mg, Cal: 230, p.38	**Grilled Chicken, Avocado, and Mixed Greens Salad** Chol: 65 mg, Cal: 290, p.83
30	**Berry Oatmeal Breakfast Smoothie** Chol: 0mg, Cal: 220, p.112	**Tomato Basil Soup** Chol: 0mg, Cal: 100, p.27 + **Chicken Mini Meatballs** Chol: 90mg, Cal: 250, p.65	**Mediterranean Farro Salad** Chol: 15mg, Cal: 300, p.85

Please note that while all recipes have been designed with a low-cholesterol diet in mind, the provided Meal Plan serves as an example and should be adaptable to your taste preferences, weight, and the guidance of your healthcare provider or dietitian. In our book, you will encounter a sufficient variety of beneficial recipes to compile a Meal Plan that meets diverse taste preferences and provides a foundation for numerous days of your healthy and flavorful diet.

Conversion Tables

BASIC KITCHEN CONVERSIONS AND EQUIVALENTS

DRY MEASUREMENTS	3 TEASPOONS	1 TABLESPOON = 1/16 CUP
	6 TEASPOONS	2 TABLESPOONS = 1/8 CUP
	12 TEASPOONS	4 TABLESPOONS = 1/4 CUP
	24 TEASPOONS	8 TABLESPOONS = 1/2 CUP
	36 TEASPOONS	12 TABLESPOONS = 3/4 CUP
	48 TEASPOONS	16 TABLESPOONS = 1 CUP
LIQUID MEASUREMENTS	8 FLUID OUNCES	1 CUP = 1/2 PINT = 1/4 QUART
	16 FLUID OUNCES	2 CUPS = 1 PINT = 1/2 QUART
	32 FLUID OUNCES	4 CUPS = 2 PINTS = 1 QUART
	128 FLUID OUNCES	16 CUPS = 8 PINTS = 4 QUARTS = 1 GALLON
	1 LITER	34 FL. OUNCES
BAKING	1 CUP ALL-PURPOSE FLOUR	= 4.5 OZ
	1 CUP ROLLED OATS	= 3 OZ
	1 LARGE EGG	= 1.7 OZ
	1 CUP BUTTER	= 8 OZ
	1 CUP MILK	= 8 OZ
	1 CUP HEAVY CREAM	= 8.4 OZ
	1 CUP GRANULATED SUGAR	= 7.1 OZ
BAKING PAN CONVERSIONS	9-INCH ROUND CAKE PAN	= 12 CUPS
	10-INCH TUBE PAN	= 16 CUPS
	11-INCH BUNDT PAN	= 12 CUPS
	9-INCH SPRINGFORM PAN	= 10 CUPS
	9X5-INCH LOAF PAN	= 8 CUPS
	9-INCH SQUARE PAN	= 8 CUPS

METRIC TO US COOKING

OVEN TEMPERATURES	120°C	250°F
	160°C	320°F
	180°C	350°F
	205°C	400°F
	220°C	425°F

BAKING IN GRAMS	1 CUP FLOUR	140 GRAMS
	1 CUP SUGAR	150 GRAMS
	1 CUP POWDERED SUGAR	160 GRAMS
	1 CUP HEAVY CREAM	235 GRAMS
VOLUME	1 MILLILITER	1/5 TEASPOON
	5 ML	1 TEASPOON
	15 ML	1 TABLESPOON
	240 ML	1 CUP OR 8 FLUID OUNCES
	1 LITER	34 FL. OUNCES
WEIGHT	1 GRAM	= .035 OUNCES
	100 GRAMS	= 3.5 OUNCES
	500 GRAMS	= 1.1 POUNDS
	1 KILOGRAM	= 35 OUNCES
COMMON CONVERSIONS	1/5 TSP	= 1 ML
	1 TSP	= 5 ML
	1 TBSP	= 15 ML
	1 FL OUNCE	= 30 ML
	1 CUP	= 237 ML
	1 PINT (2 CUPS)	= 473 ML
	1 QUART (4 CUPS)	= .95 LITER
	1 GALLON (16 CUPS)	= 3.8 LITERS
	1 OZ	= 28 GRAMS
	1 POUND	= 454 GRAMS
WHAT DOES 1 CUP EQUAL		= 8 FLUID OUNCES
		= 16 TABLESPOONS
		= 48 TEASPOONS
		= 1/2 PINT
		= 1/4 QUART
		= 1/16 GALLON
		= 240 ML
1 CUP BUTTER	= 2 STICKS = 8 OUNCES = 230 GRAMS = 8 TABLESPOONS	

Recipes Index
(in alphabetical order)

My sincere thanks to Serge Berg for his work on the design of this cookbook. He managed to make each page not only informative but also attractive. His creativity and attention to detail gave this project a special value.

Made in United States
Troutdale, OR
11/22/2024

25189455R00080